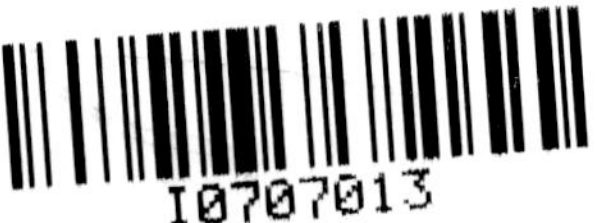

I am grateful to God for everything!
May this book open the doors to a wonderful, magical and colorful world.

KELLY CAVALCANTE
2024

This Book Belongs to:

____

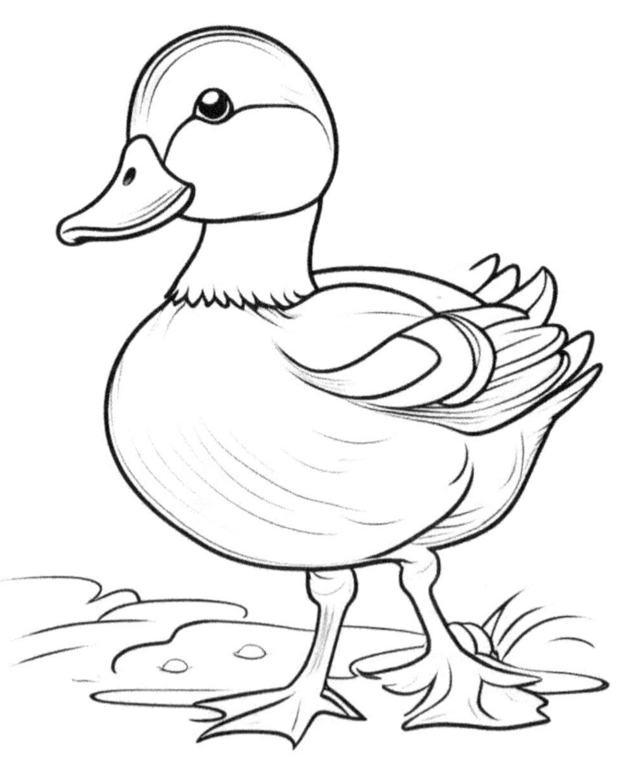

Test Color Page

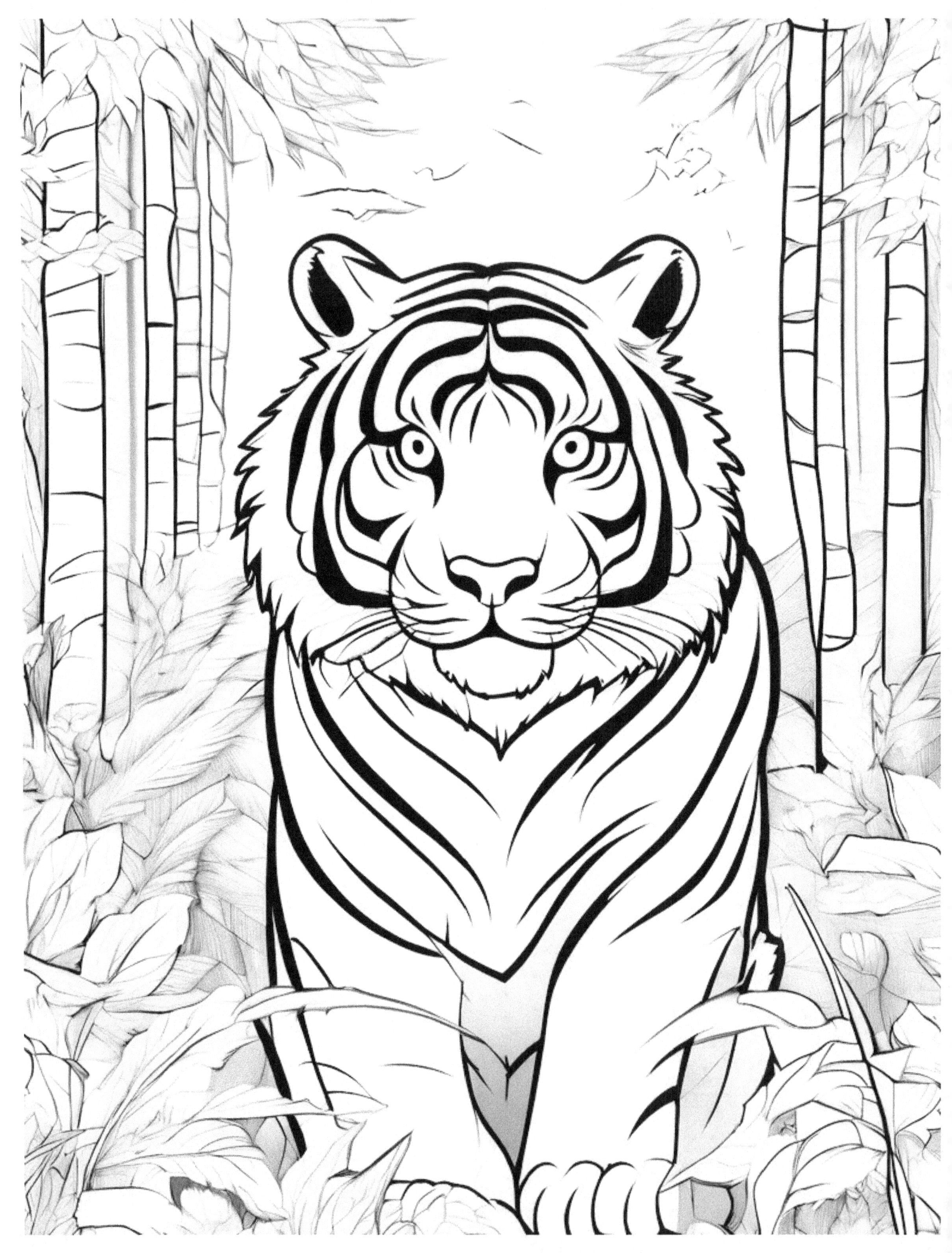

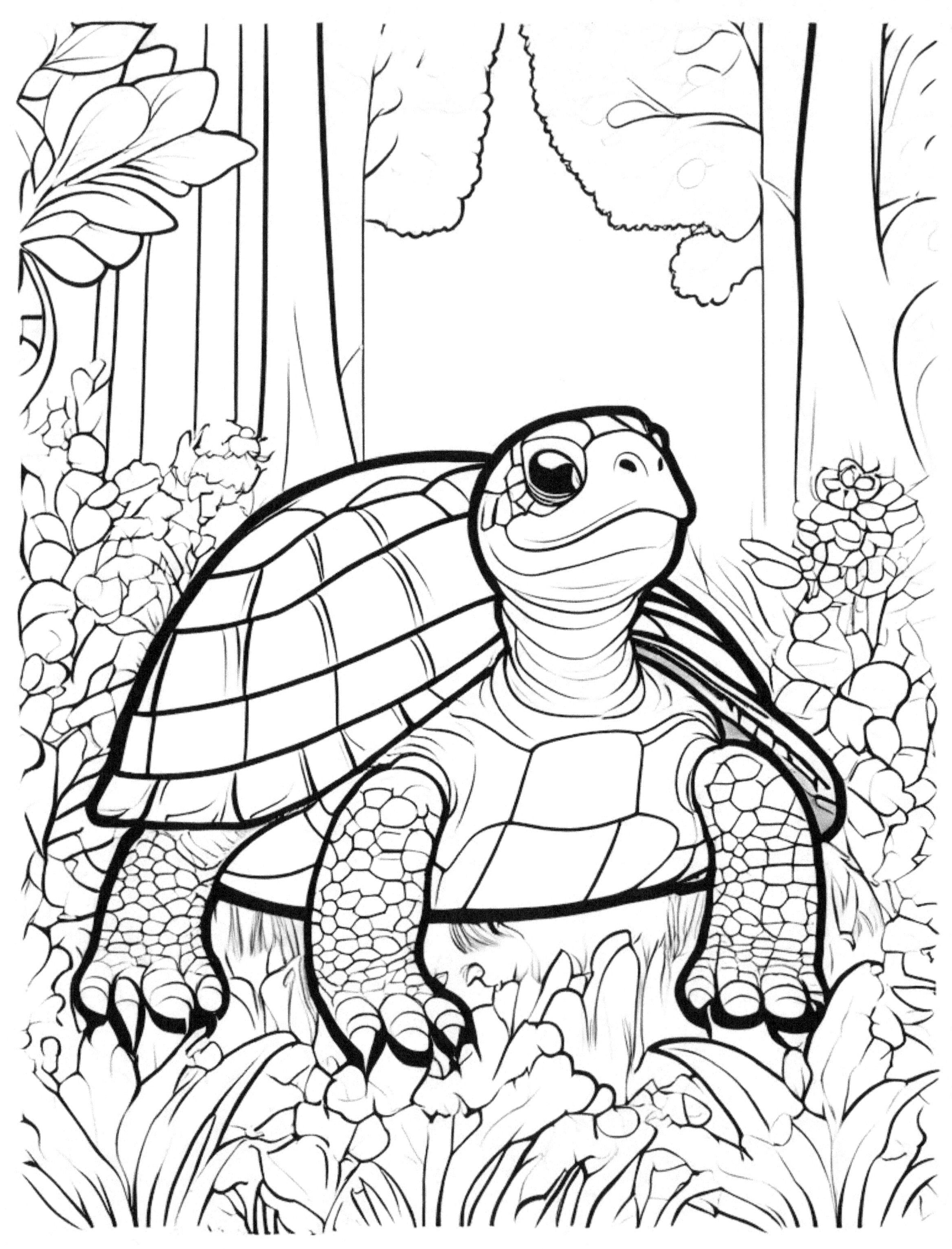

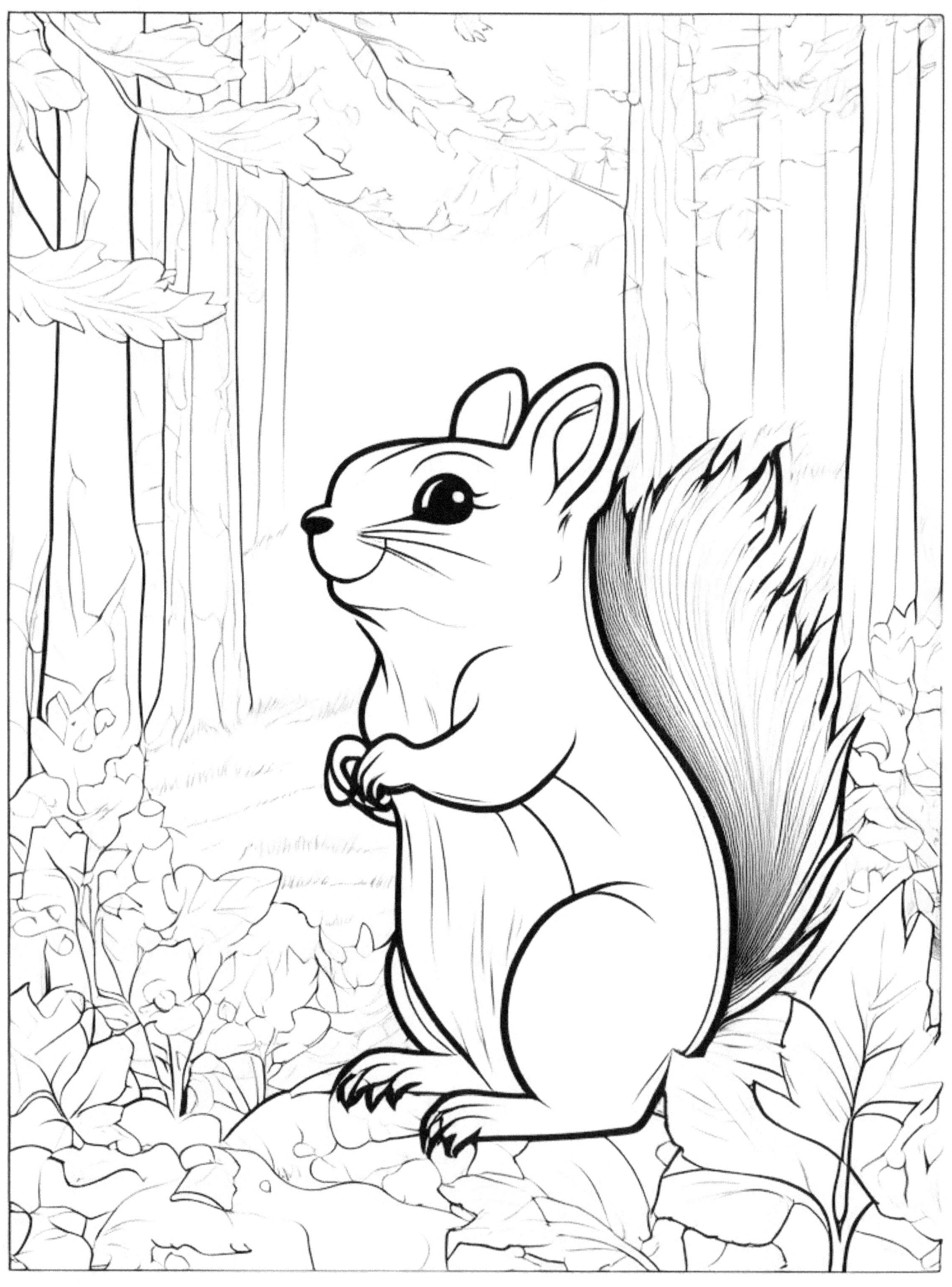

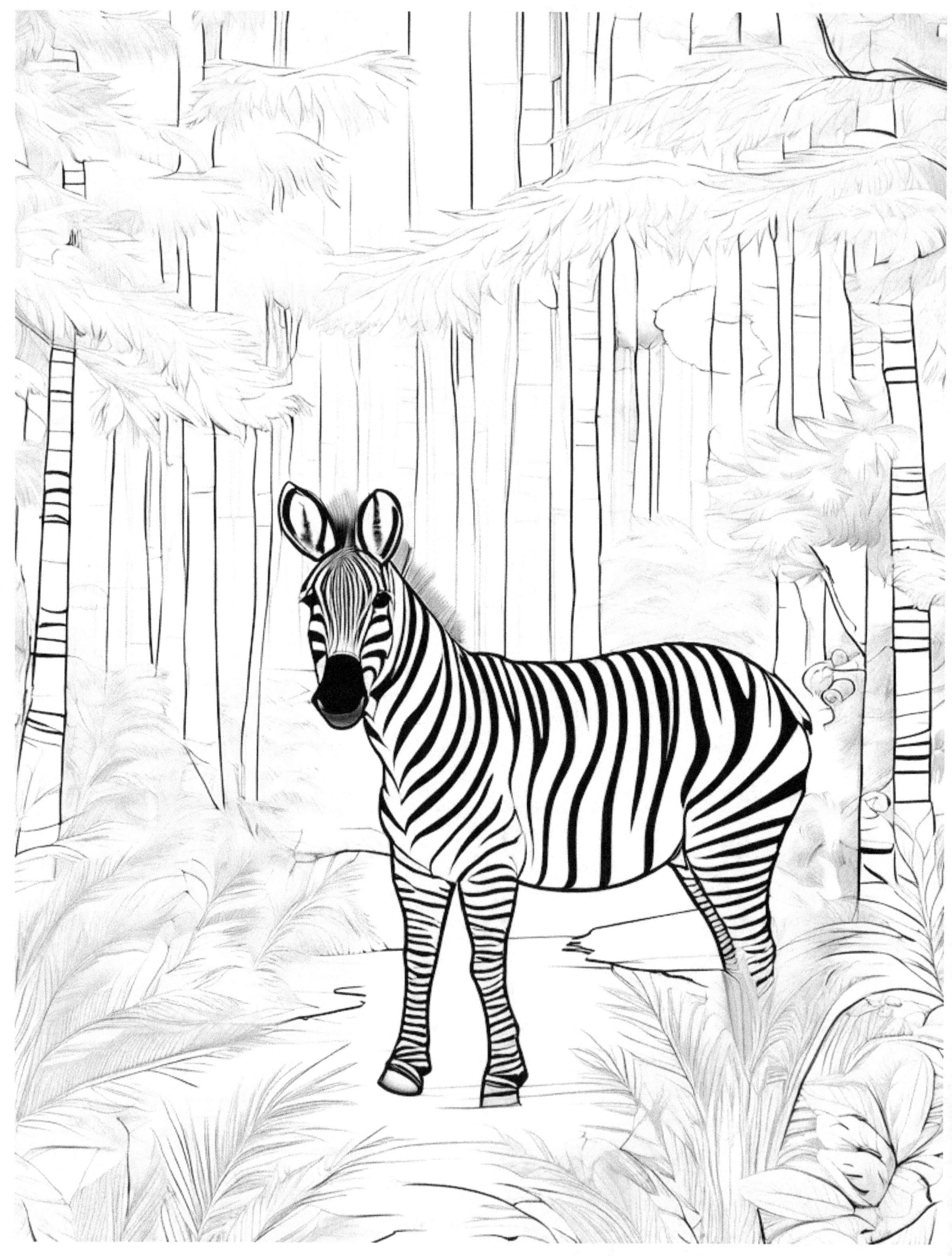

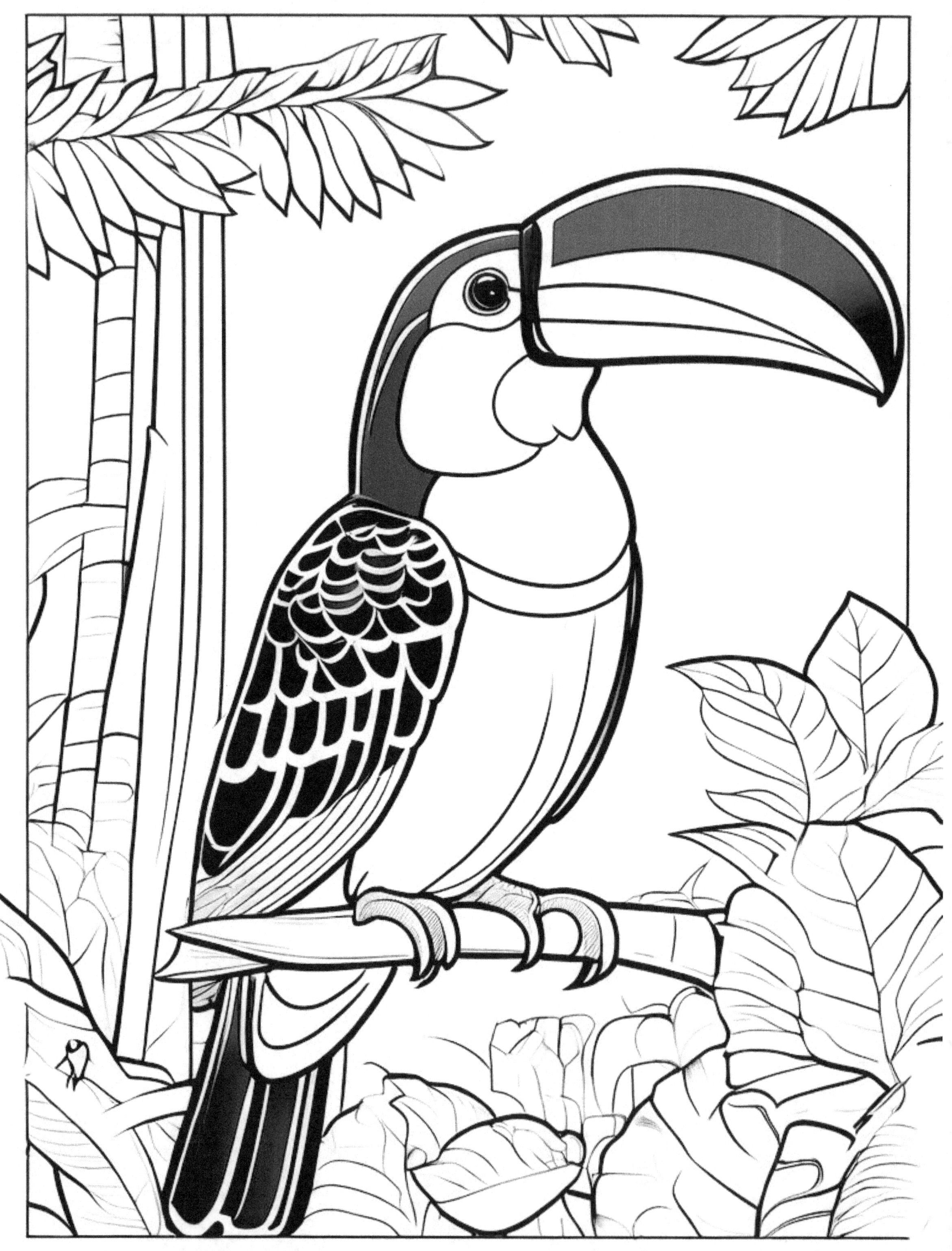

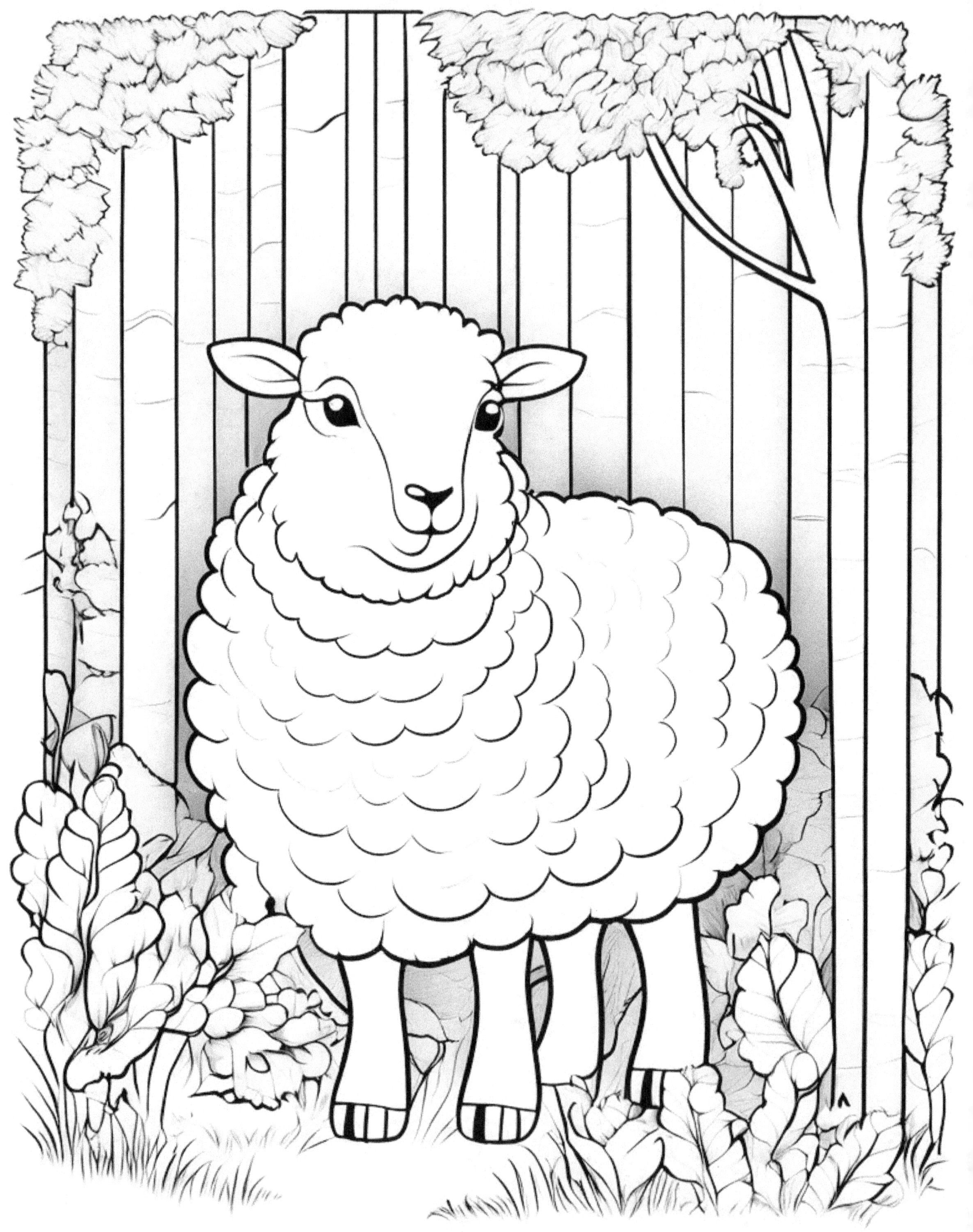

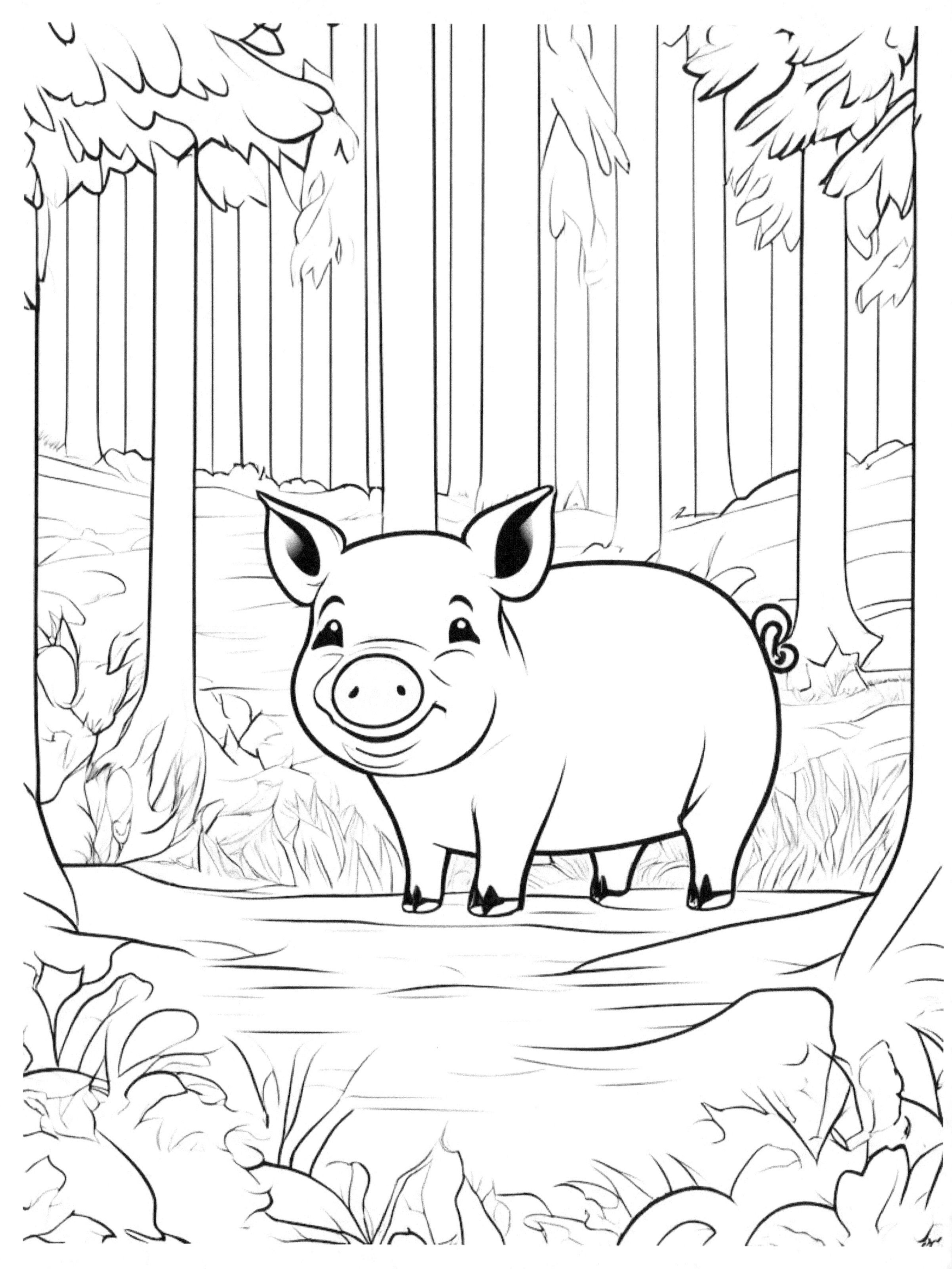

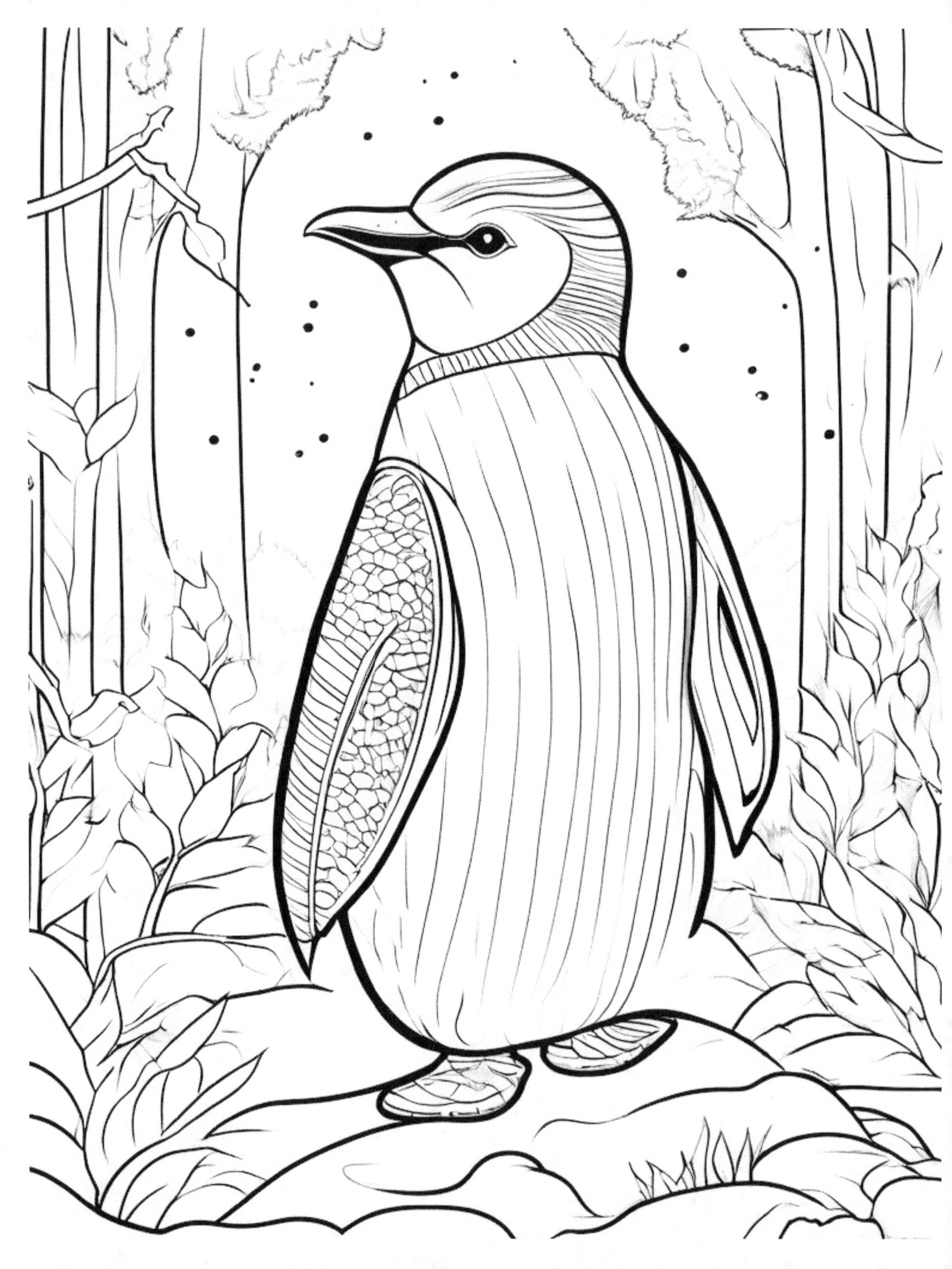

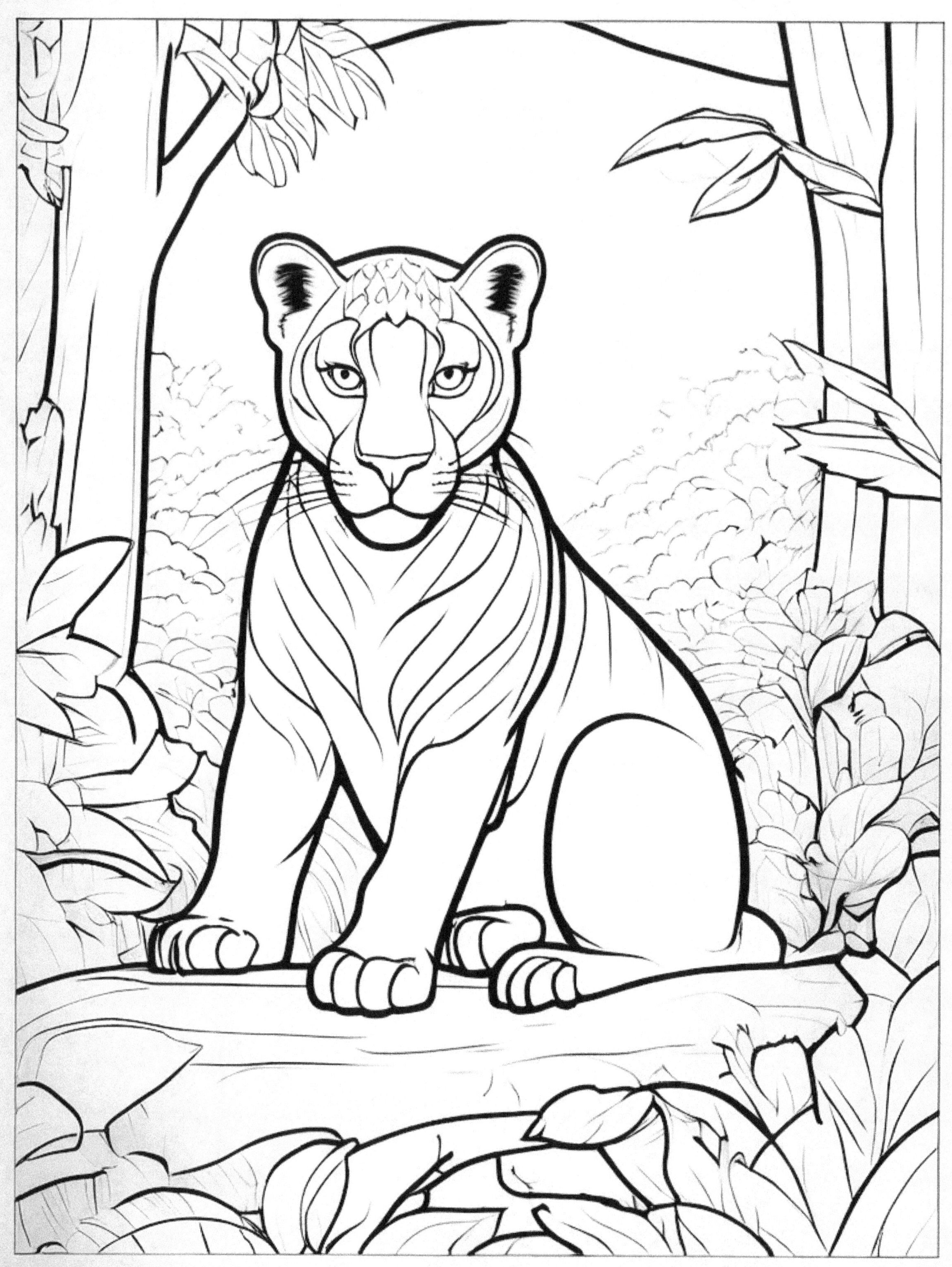

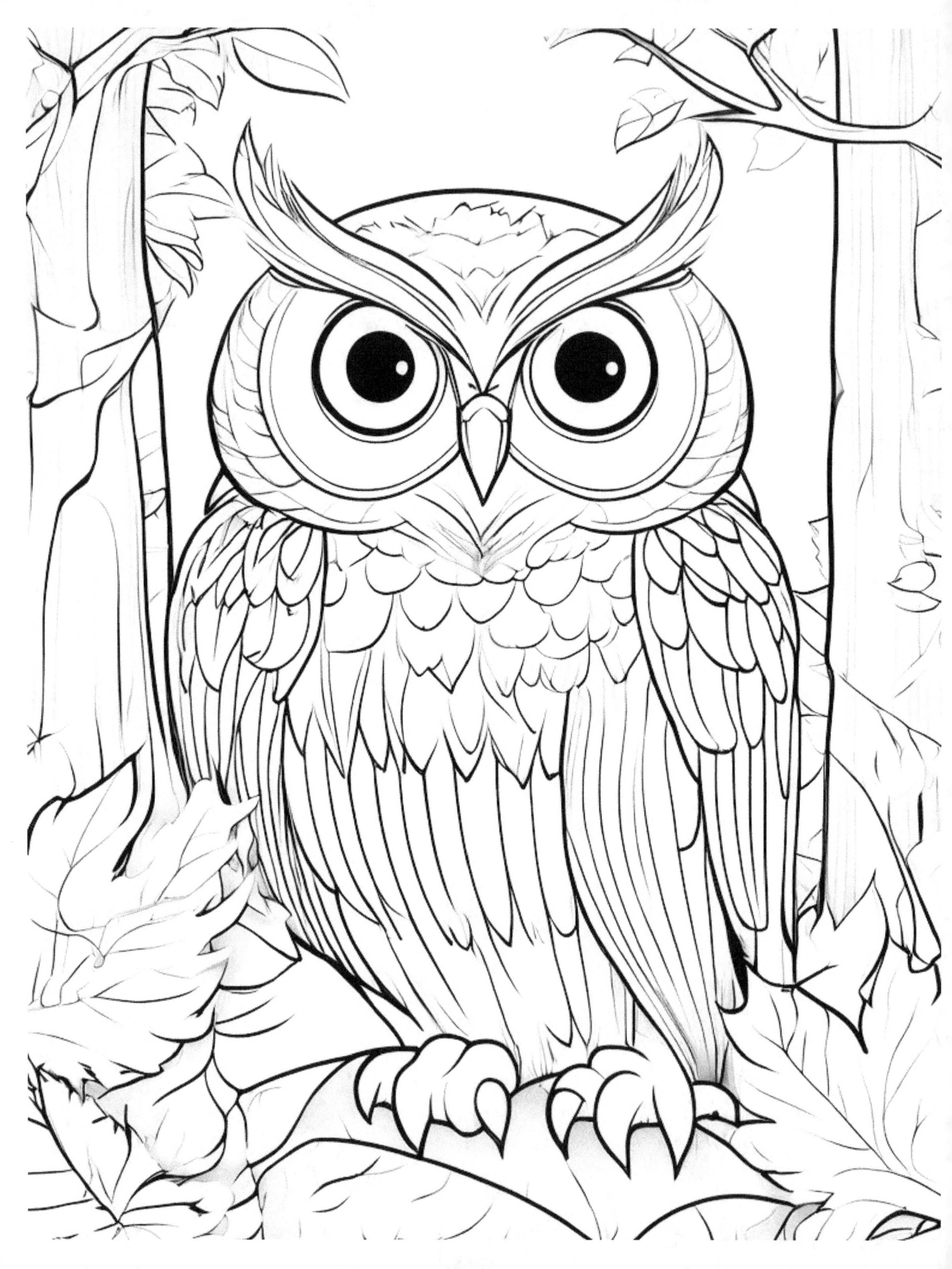

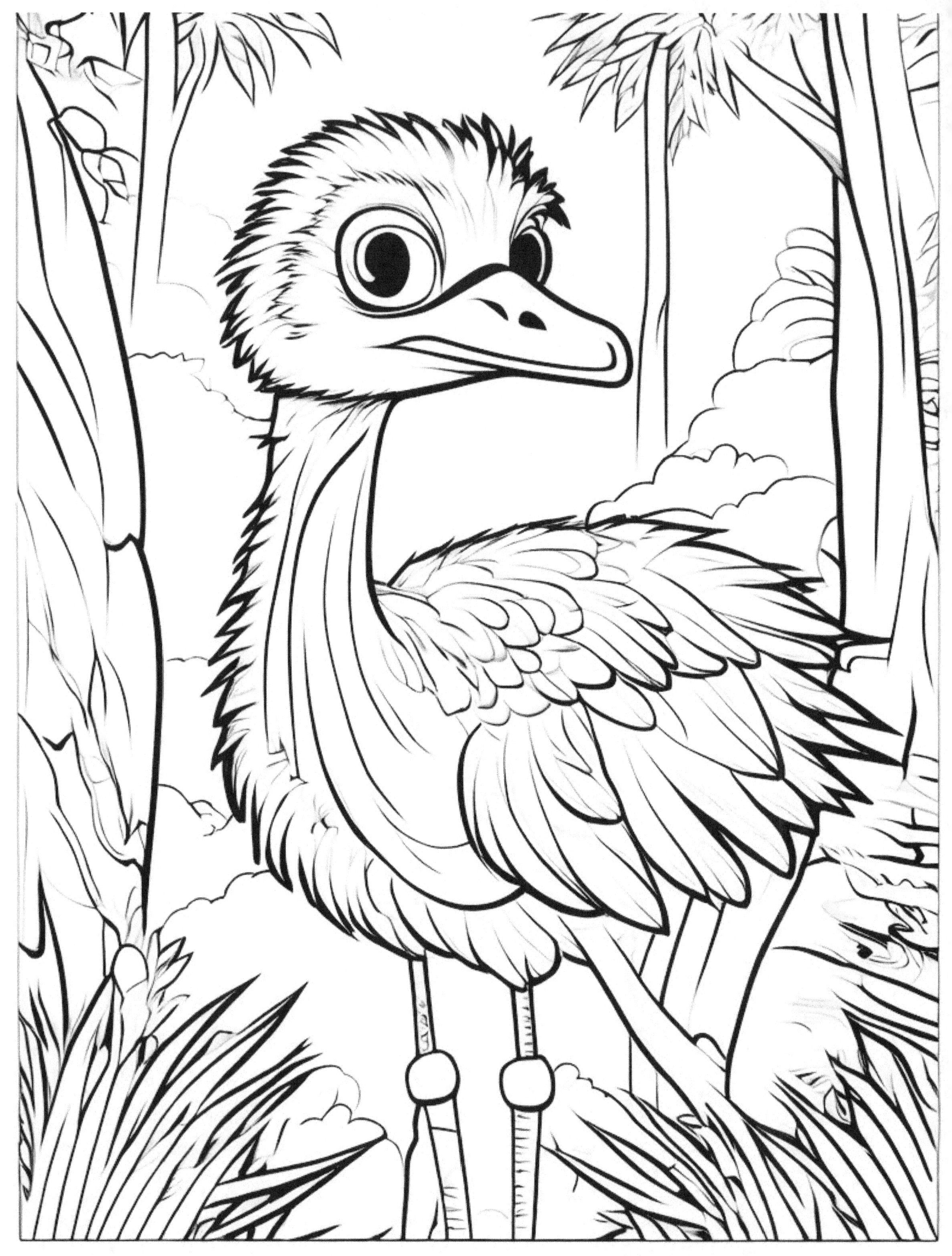

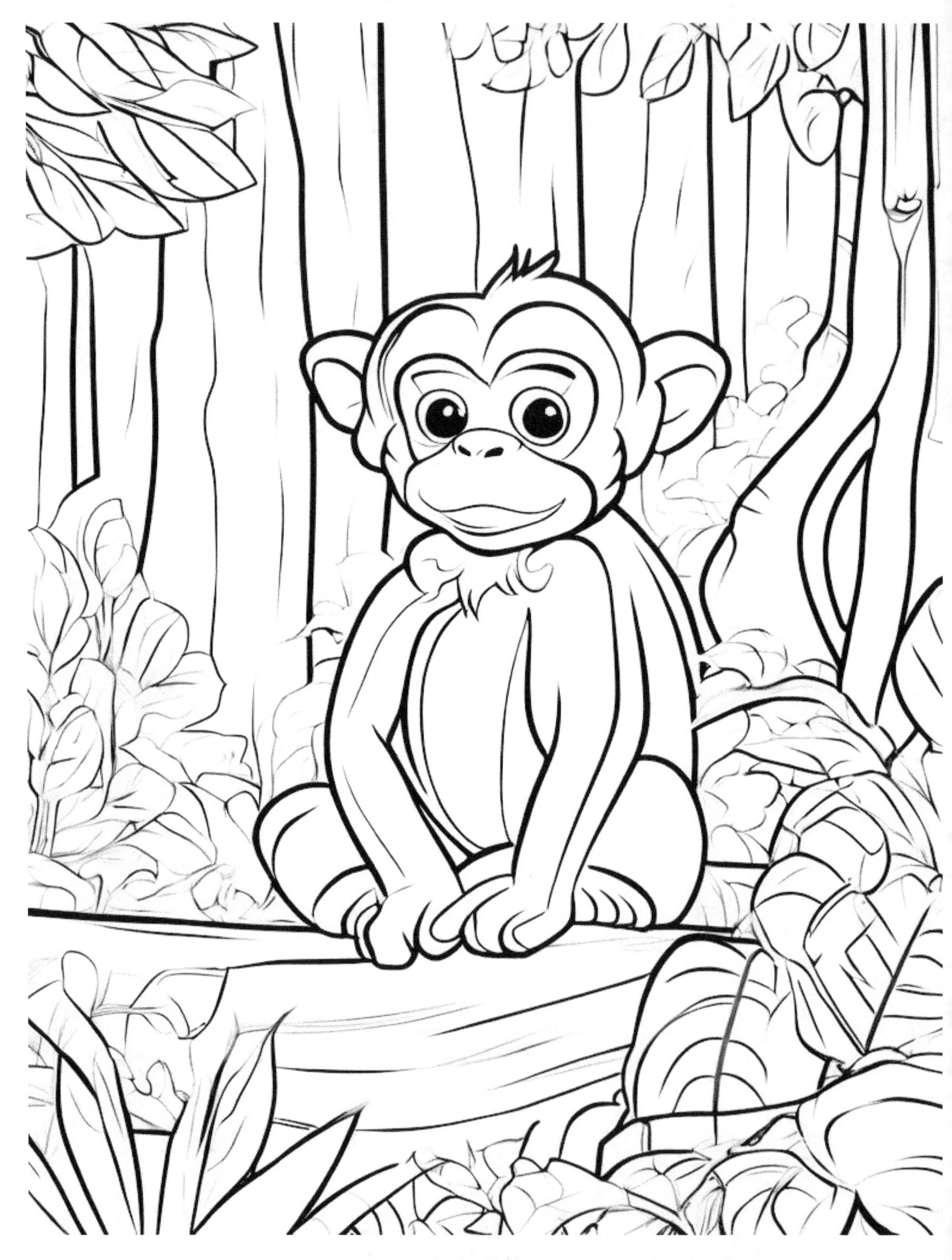

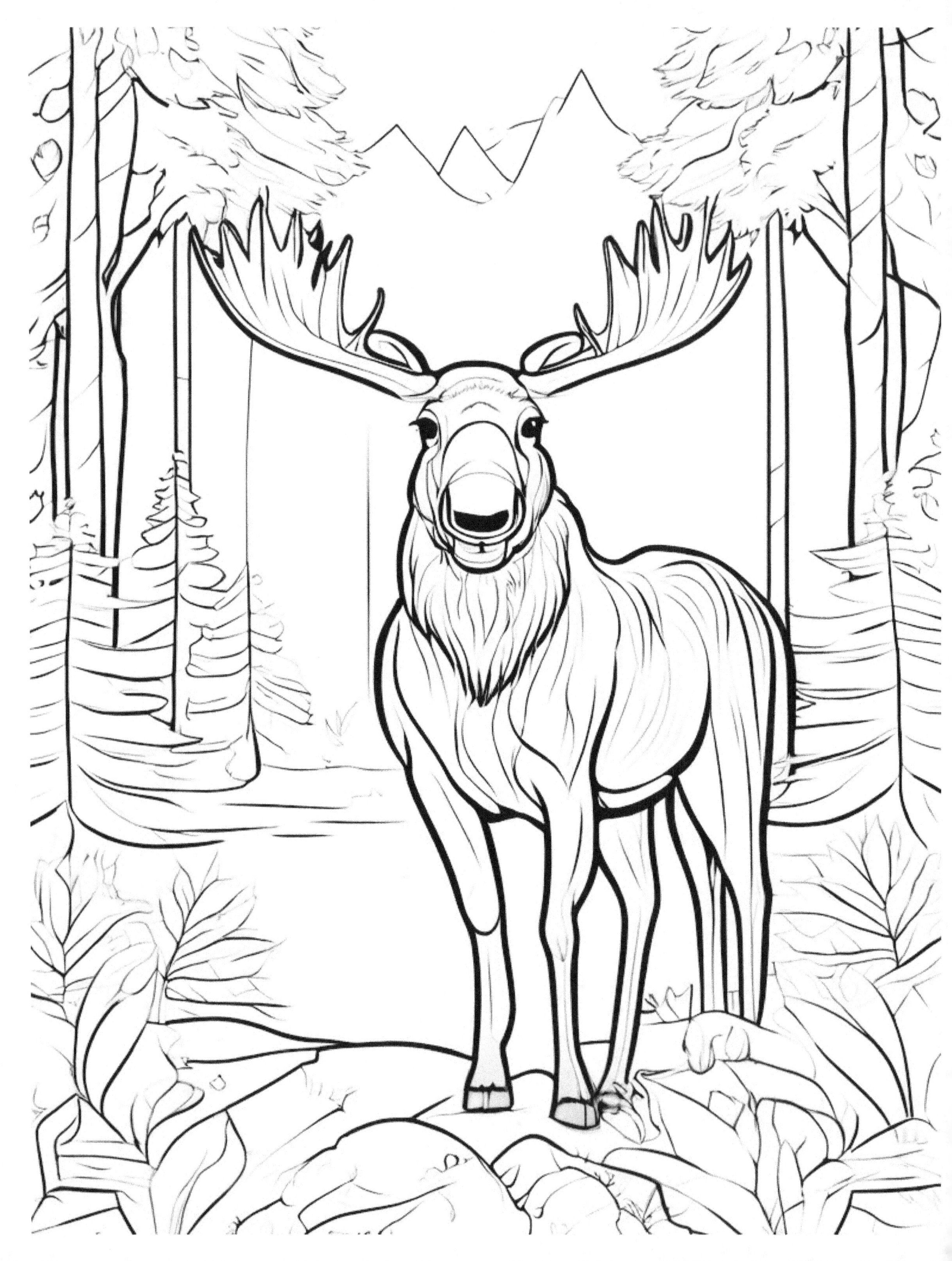

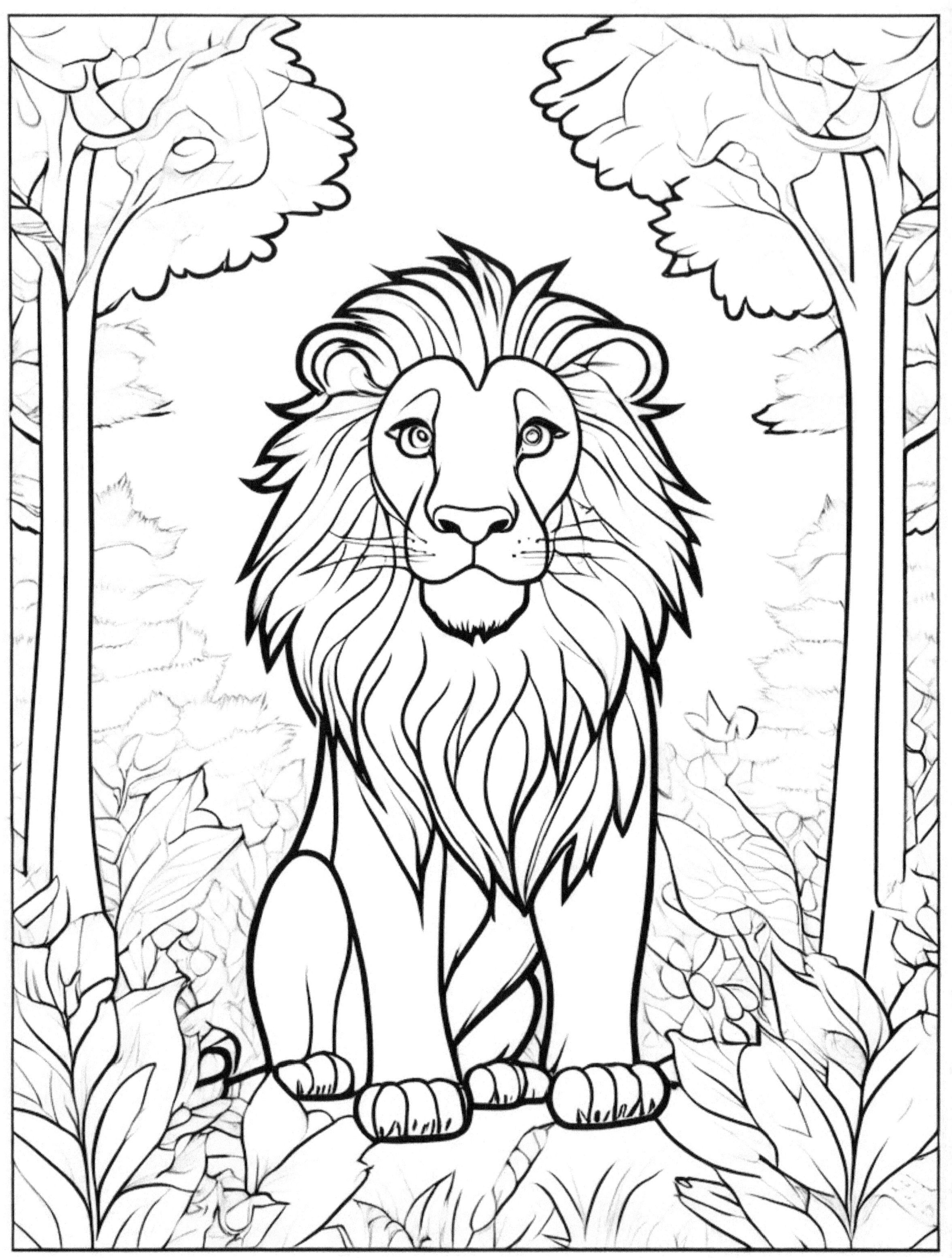

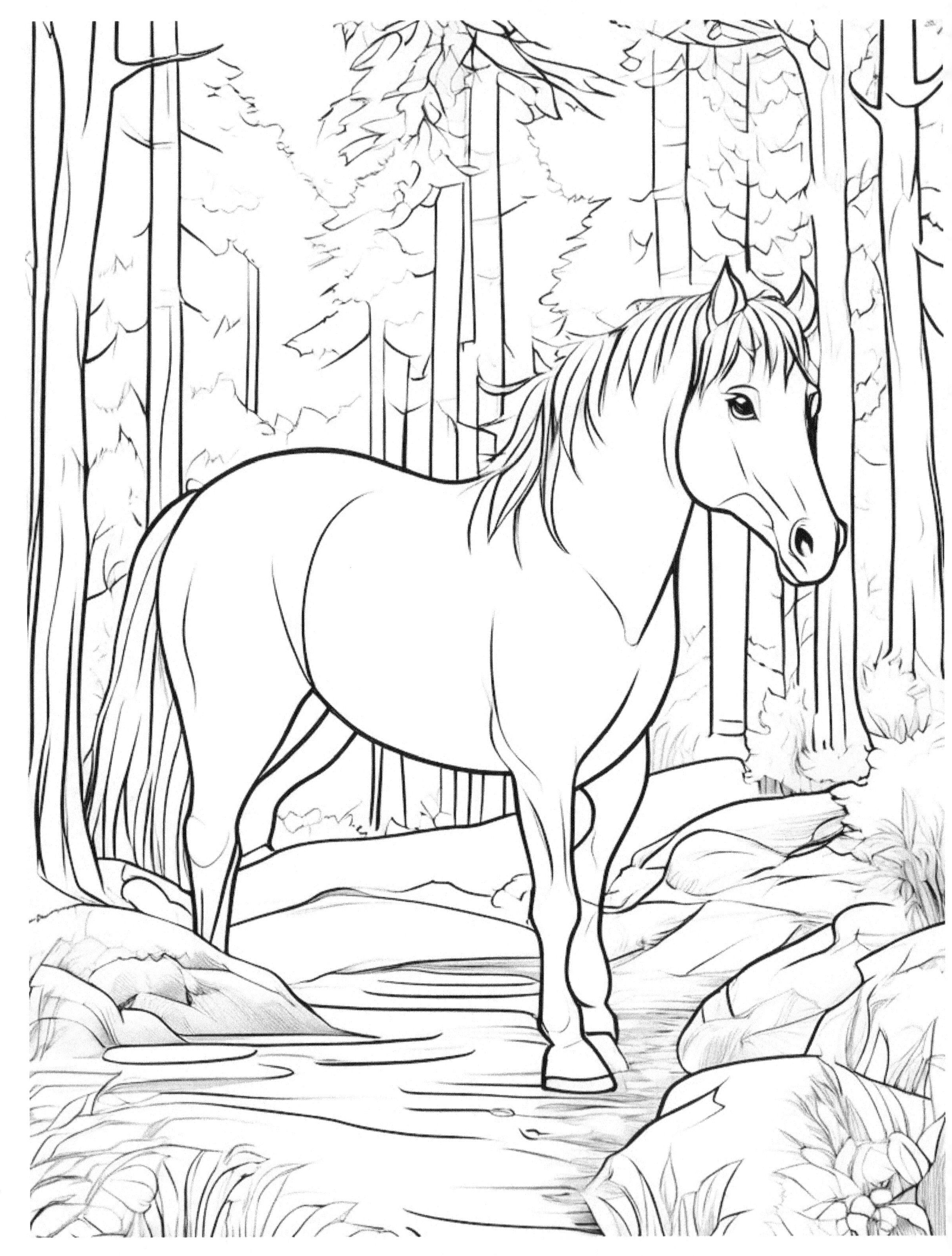

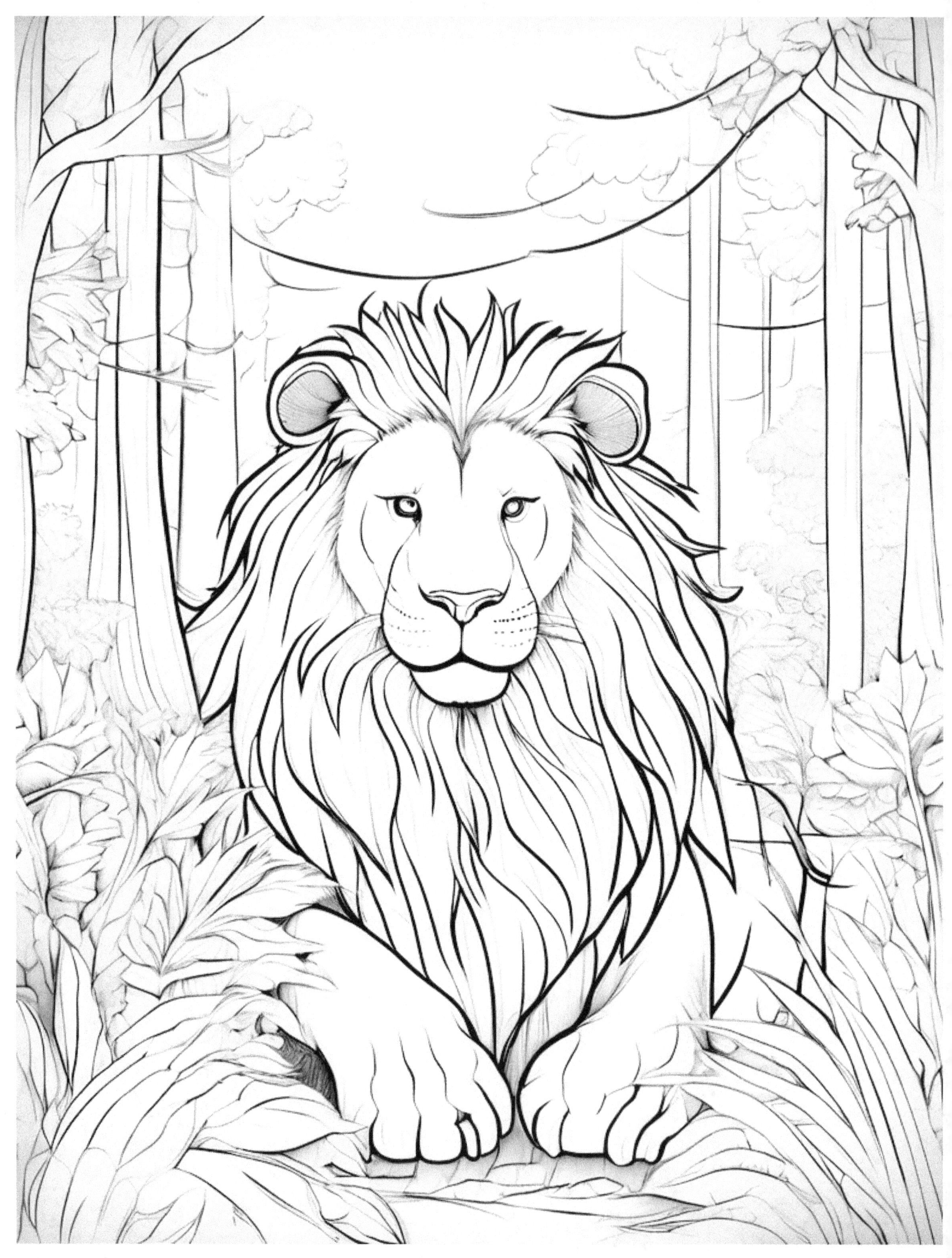

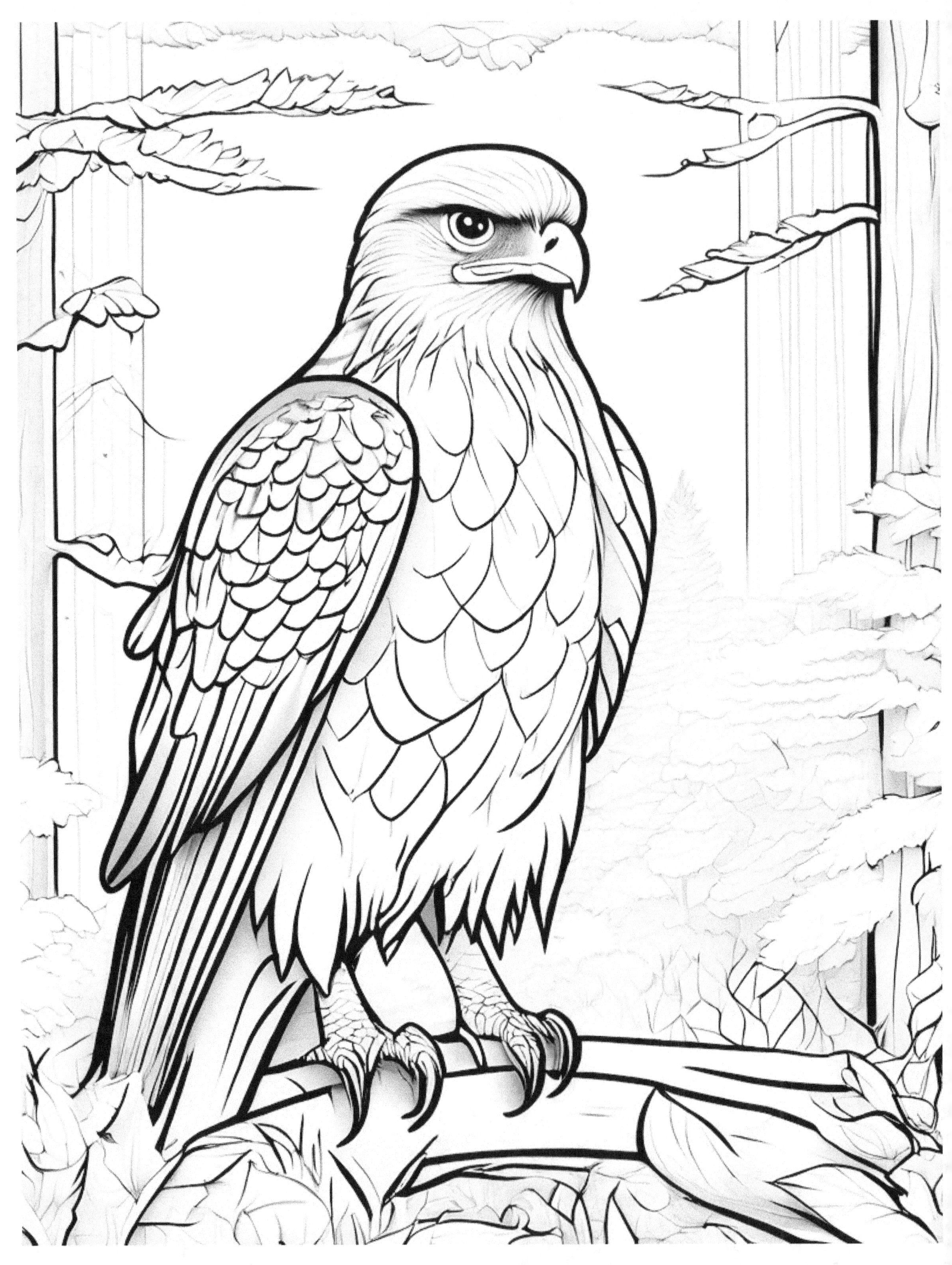

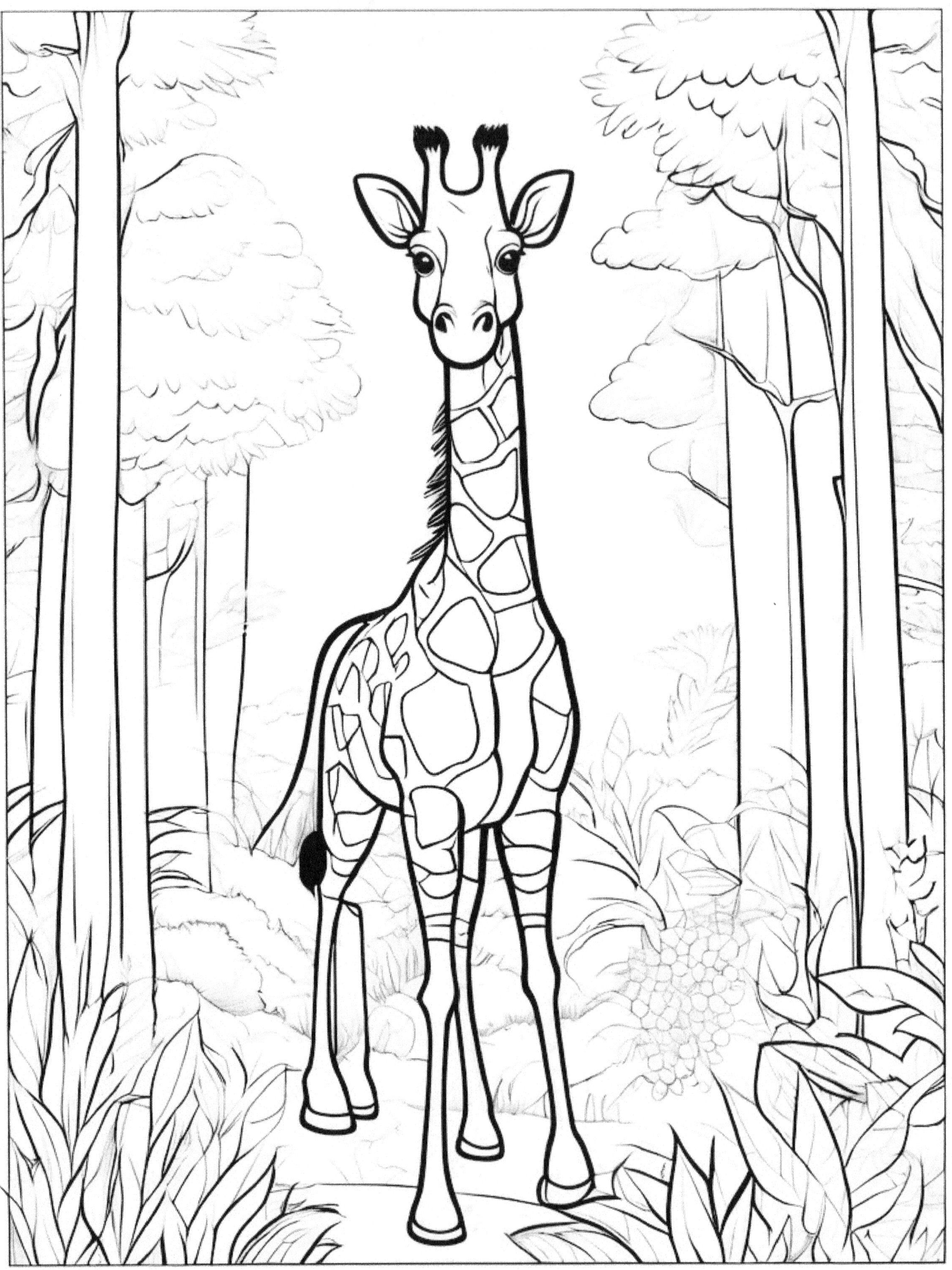

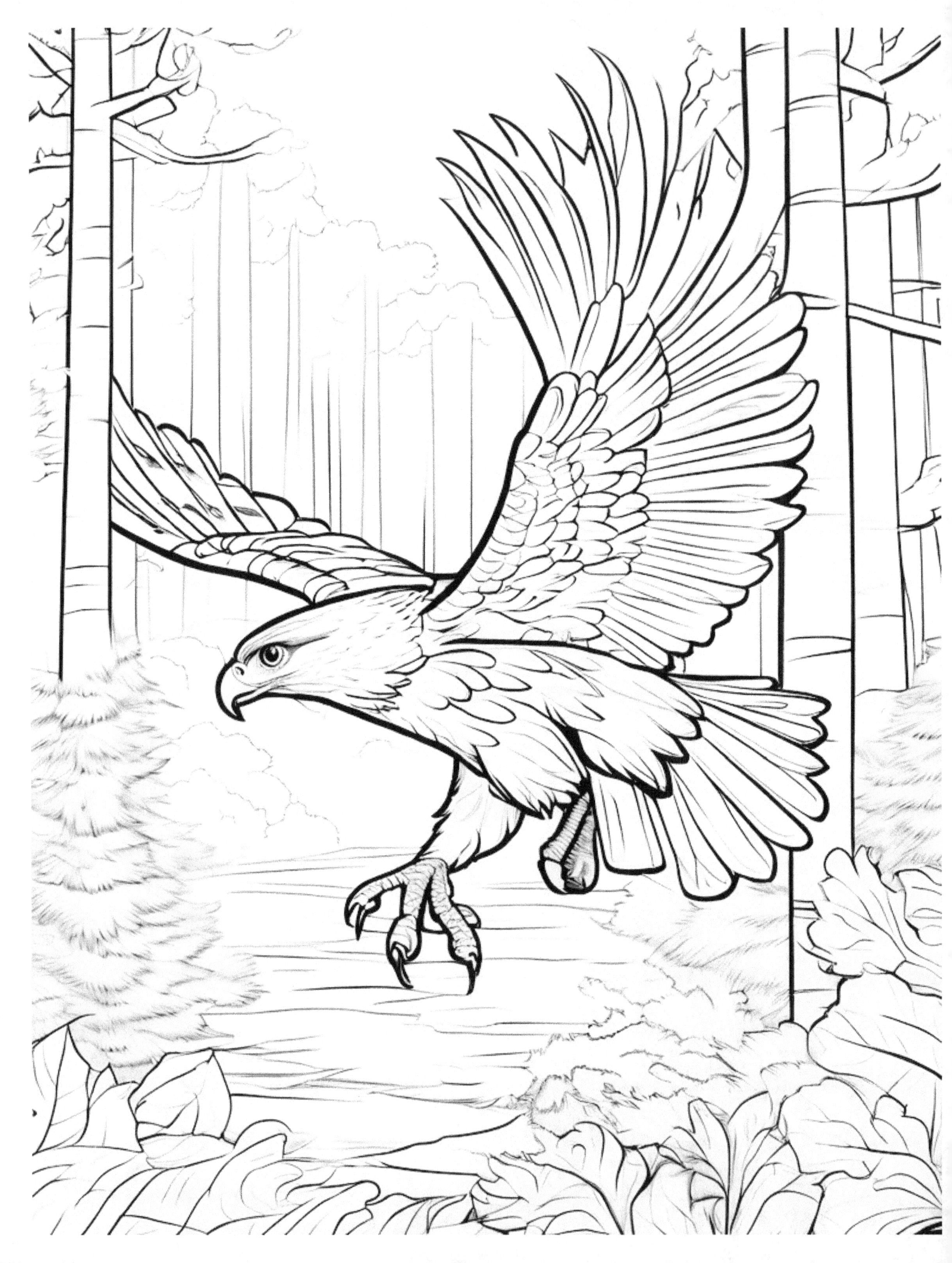

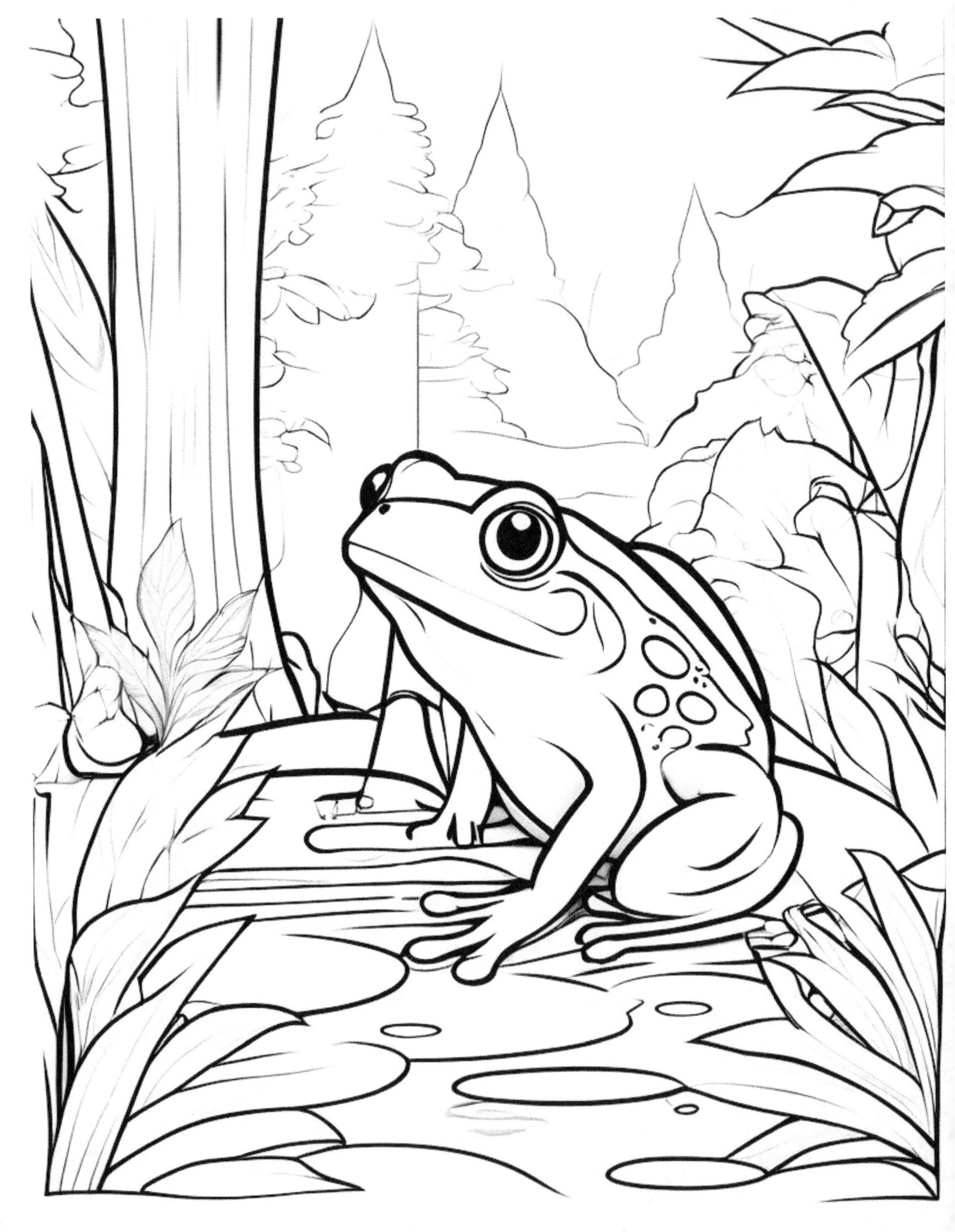

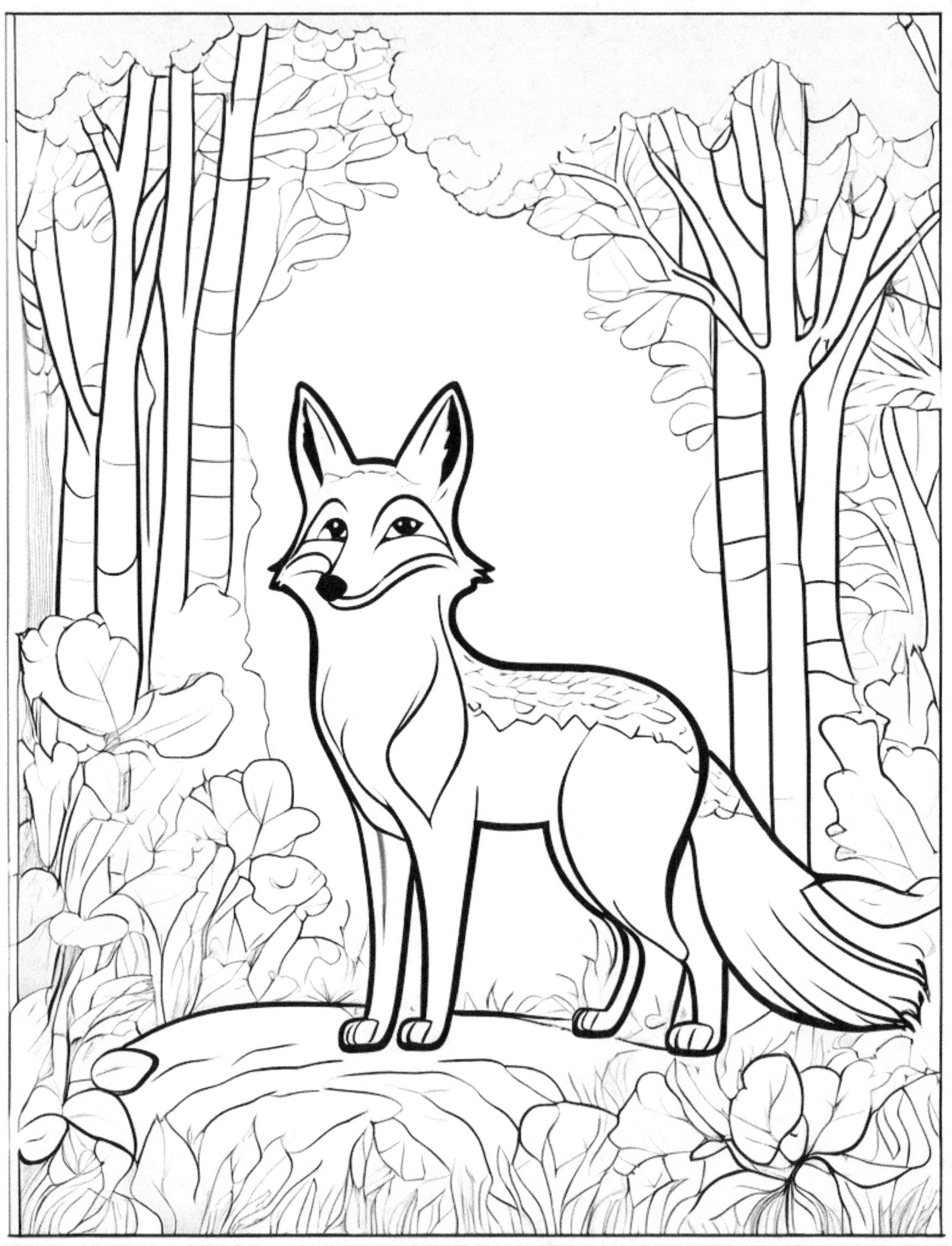

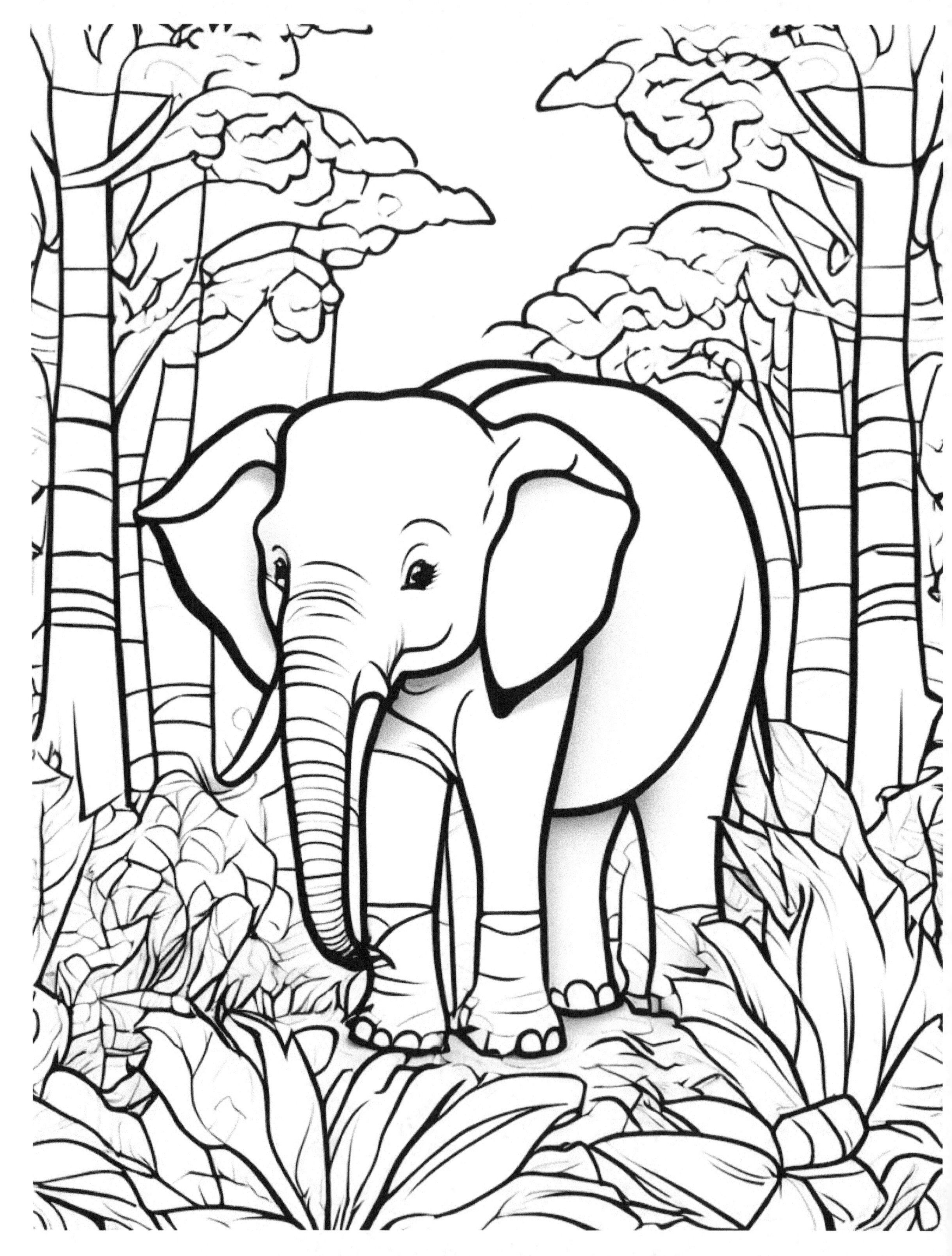

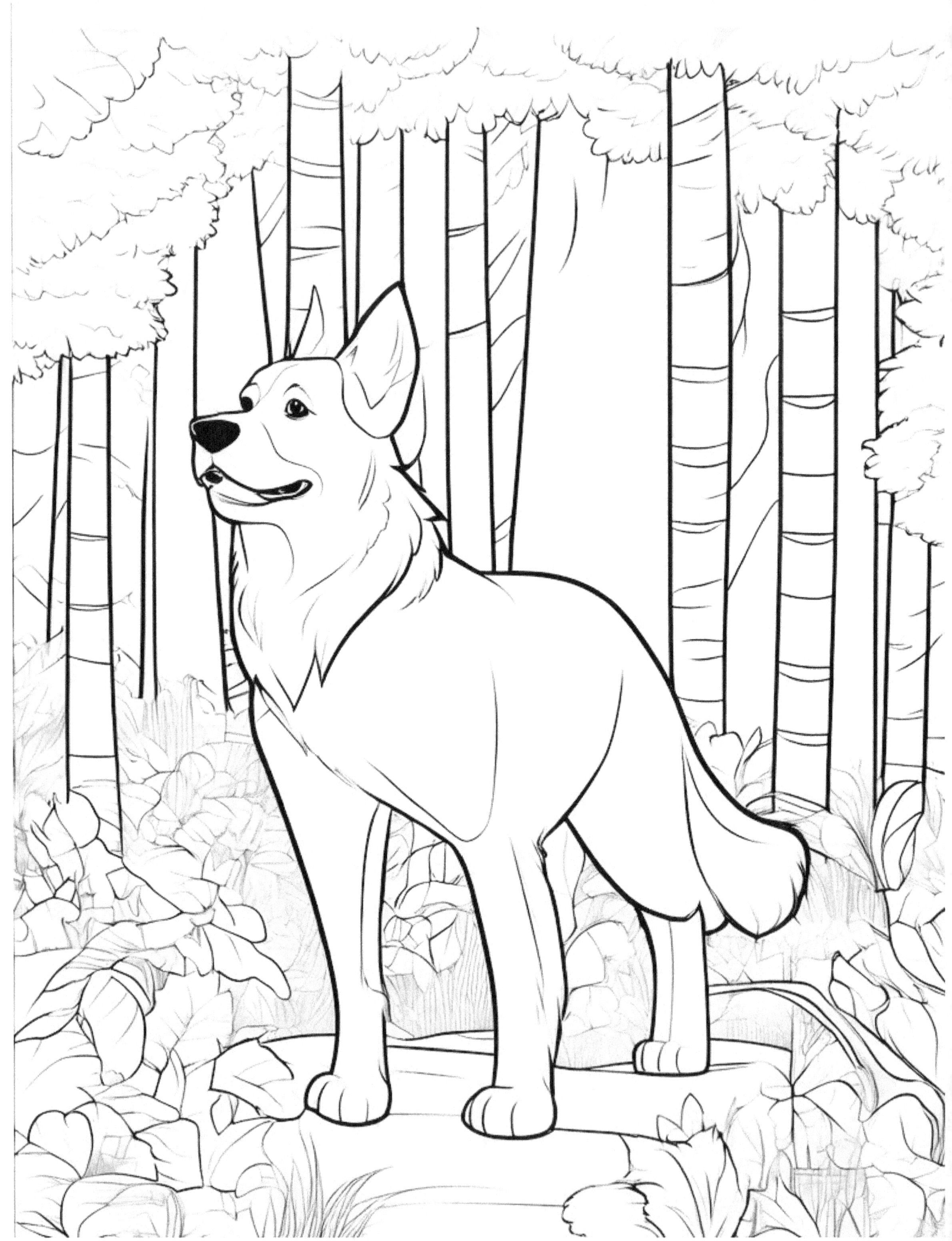

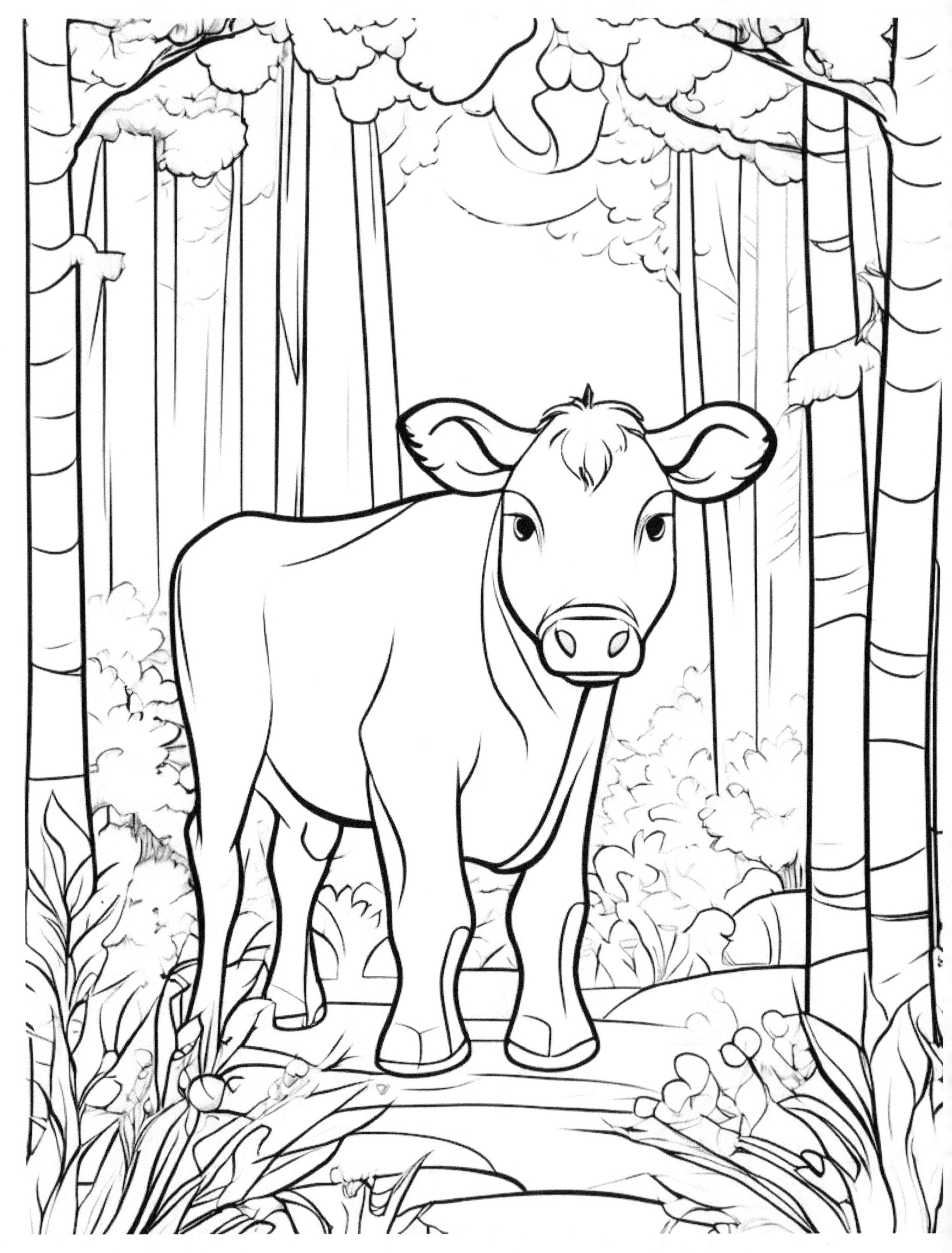

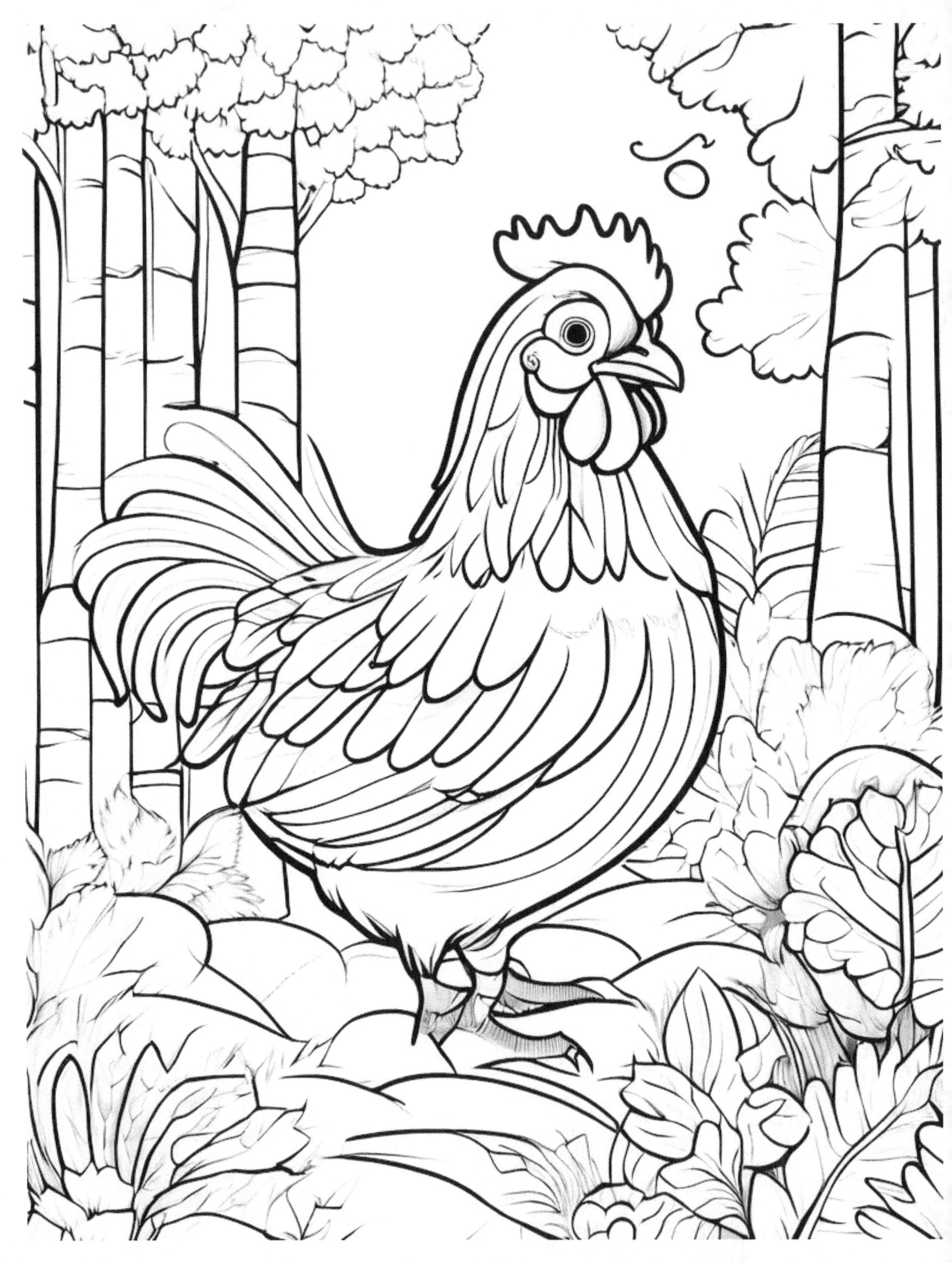

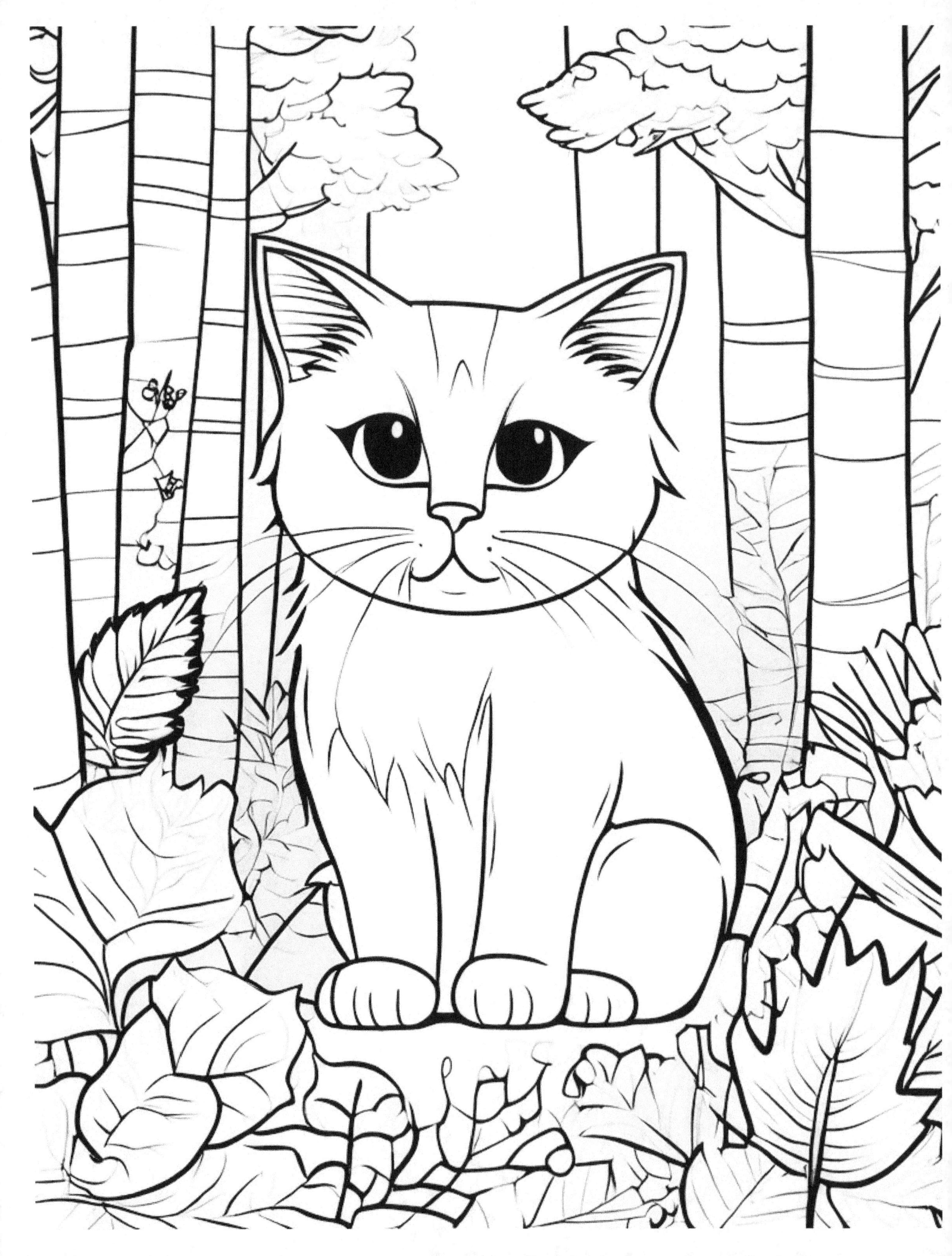

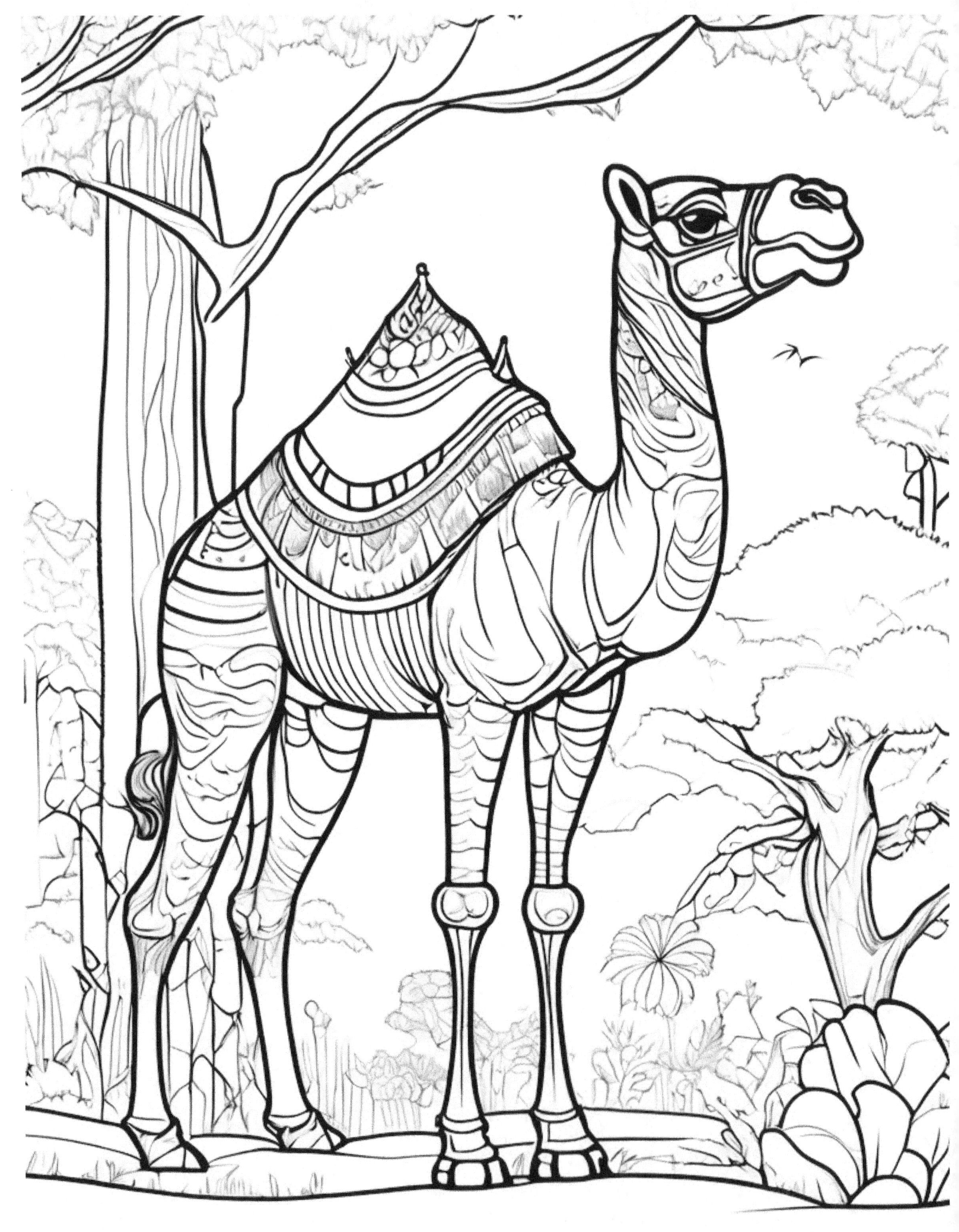

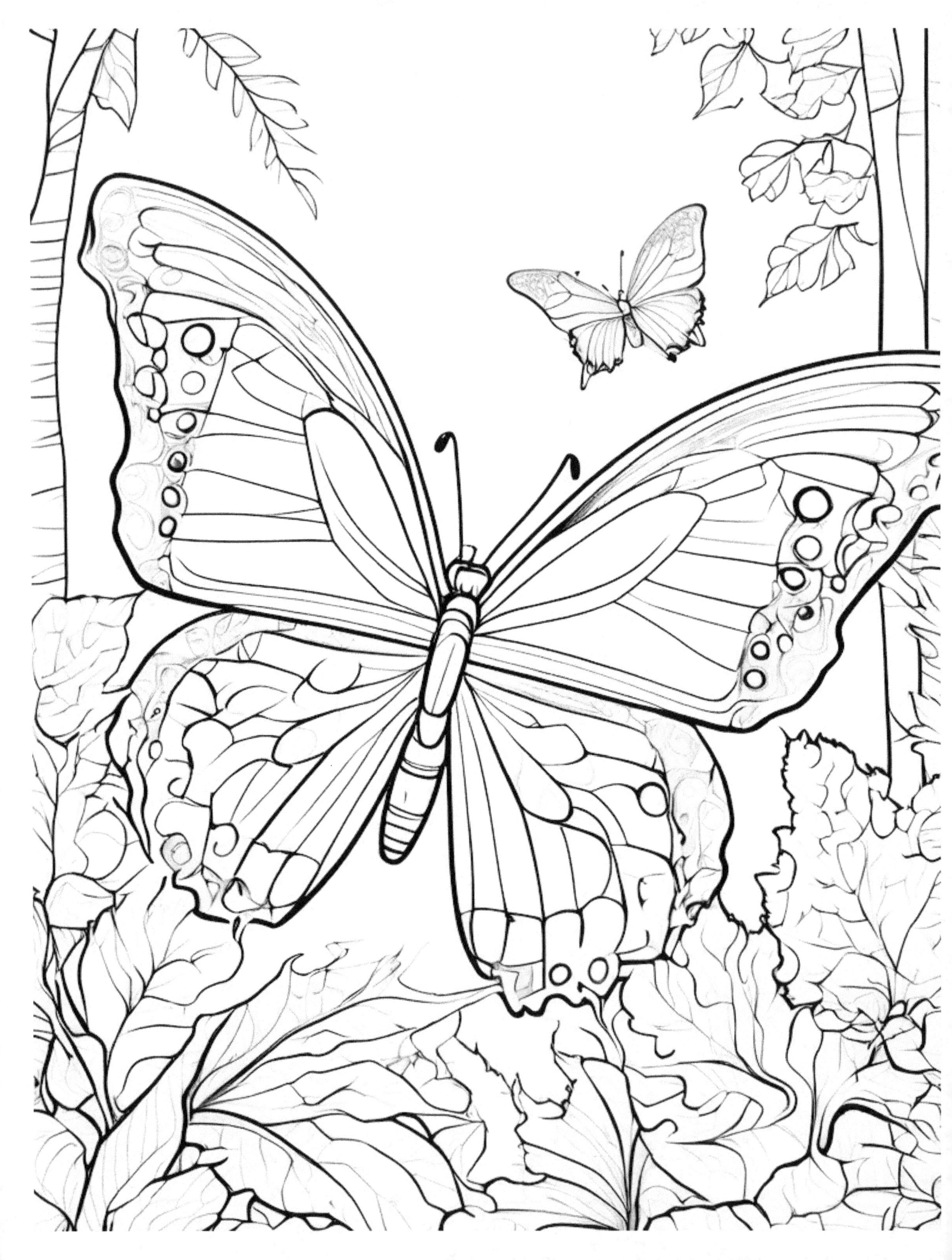

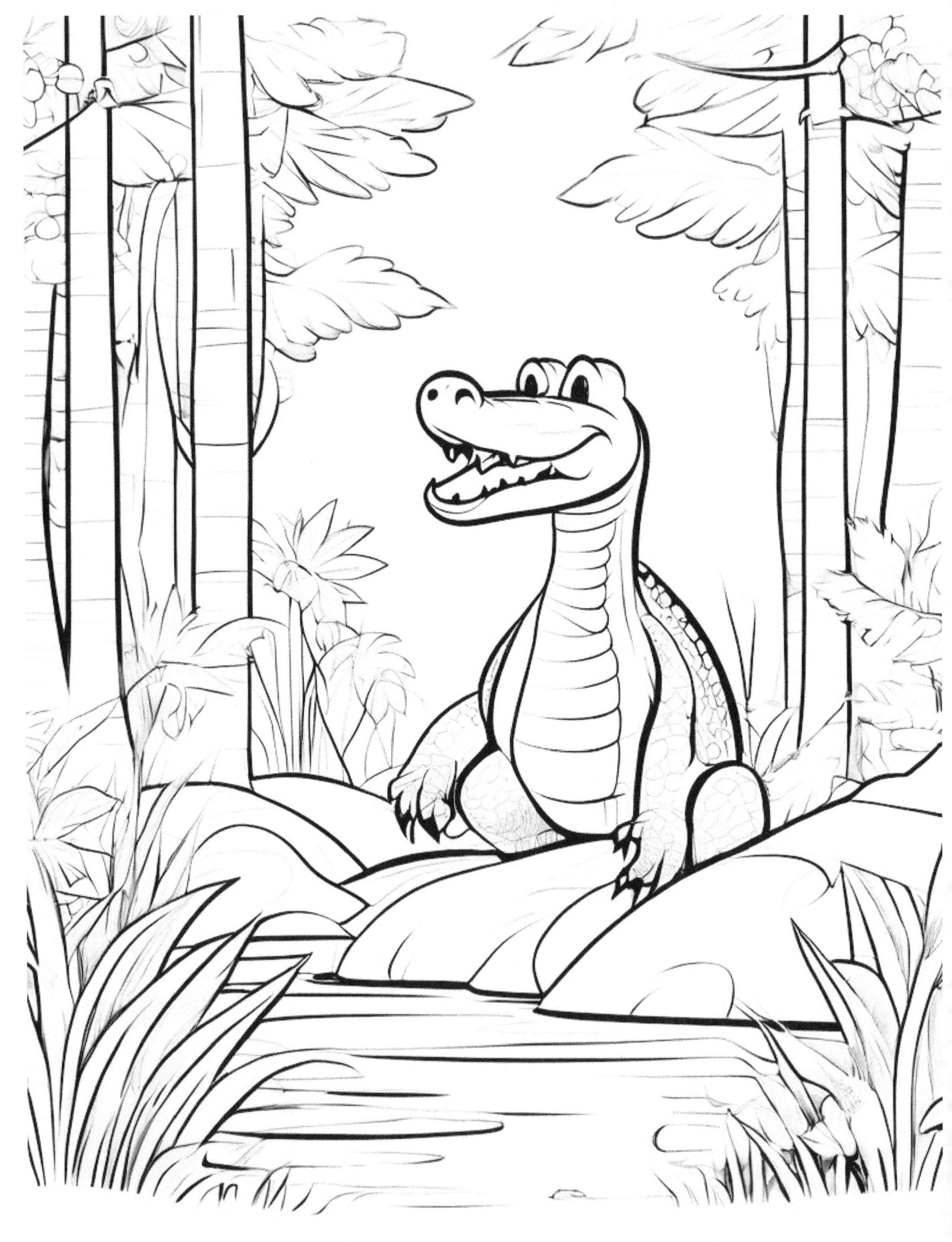

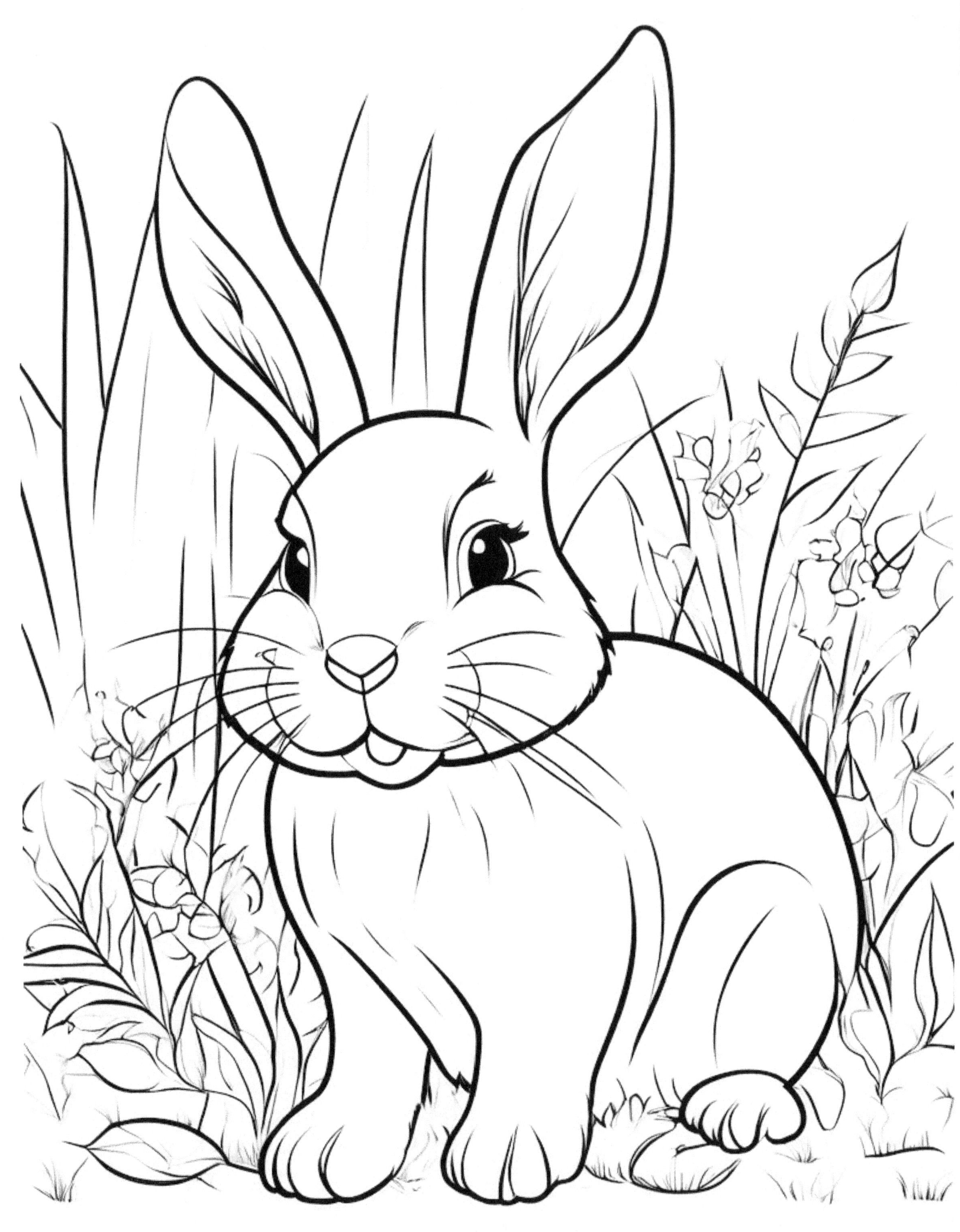

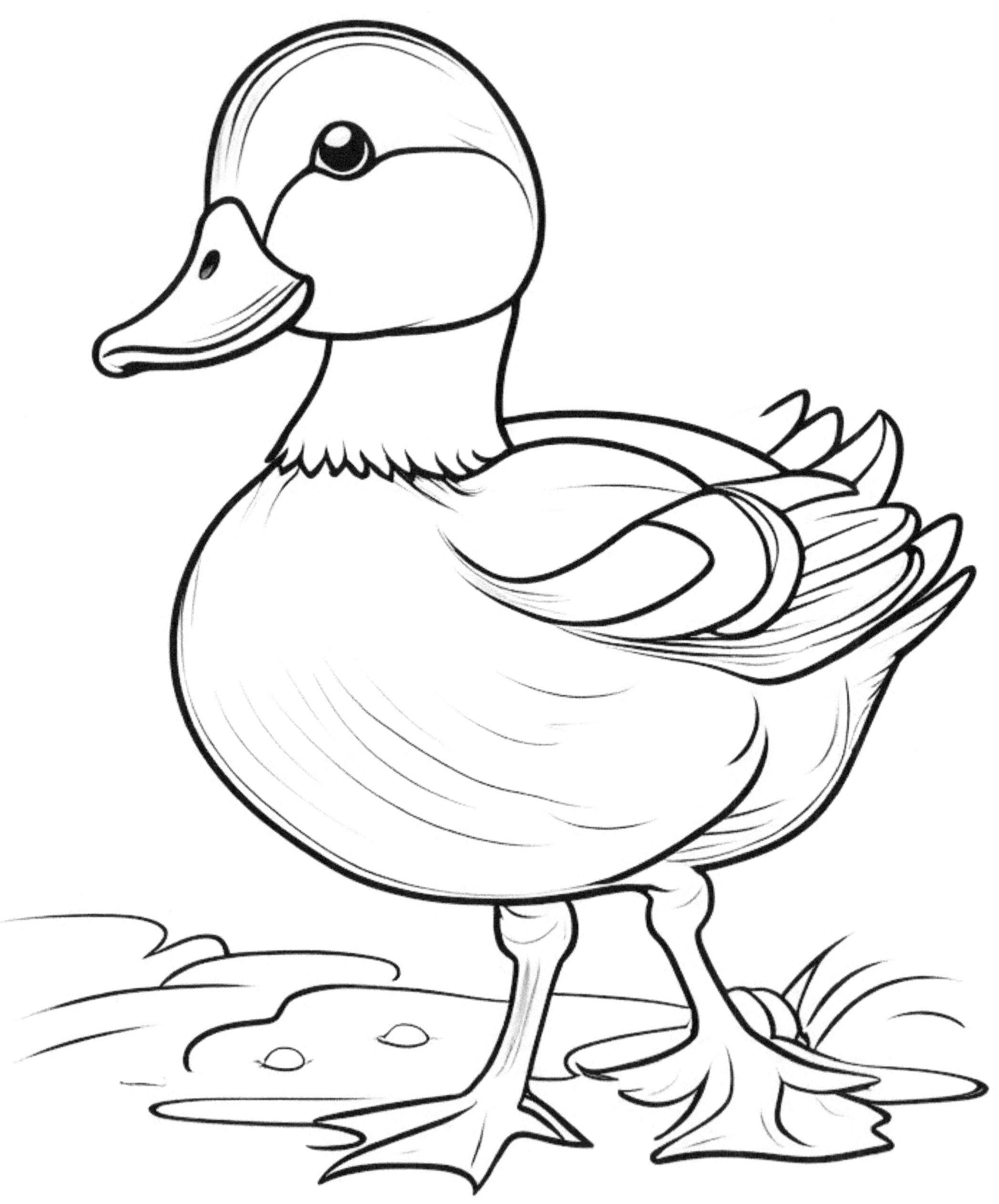

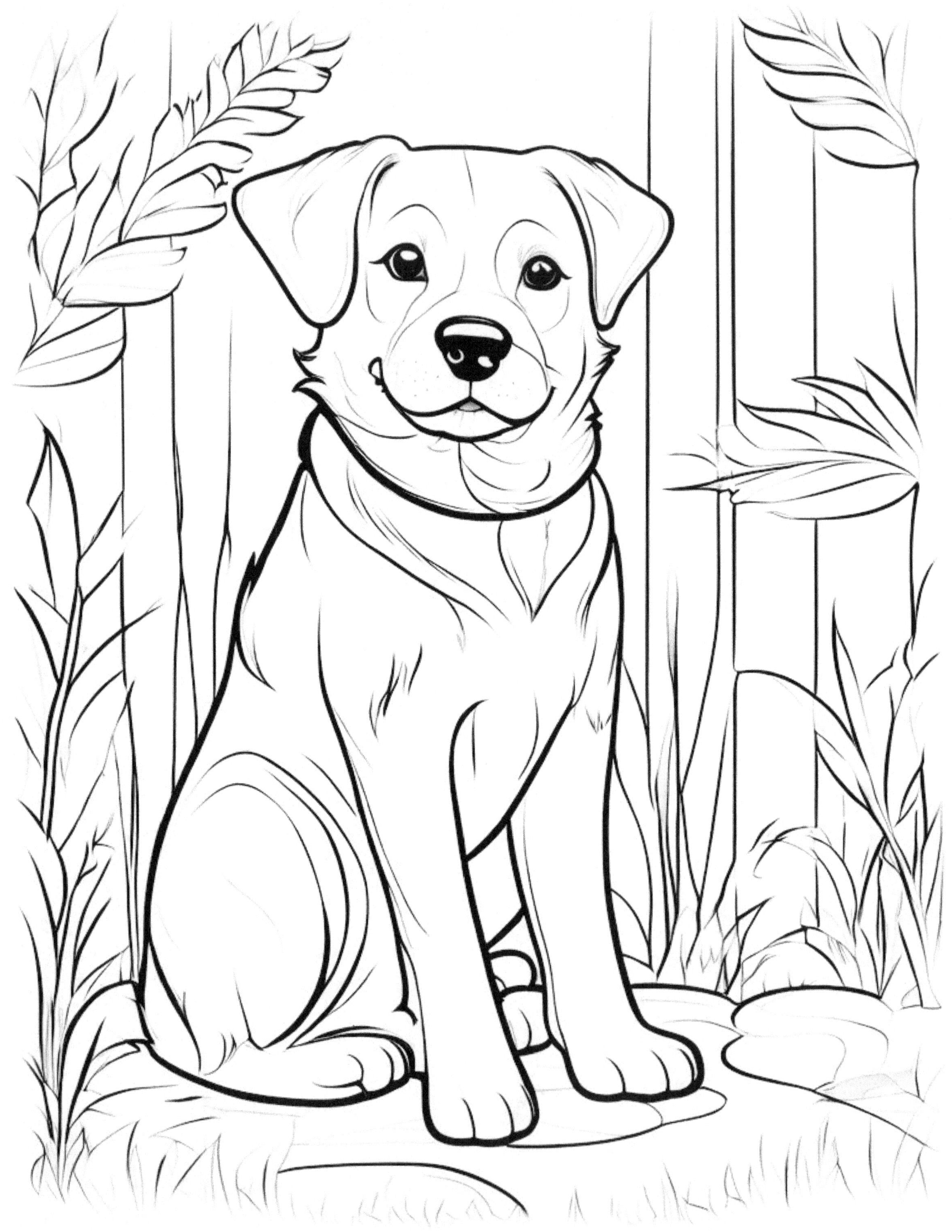

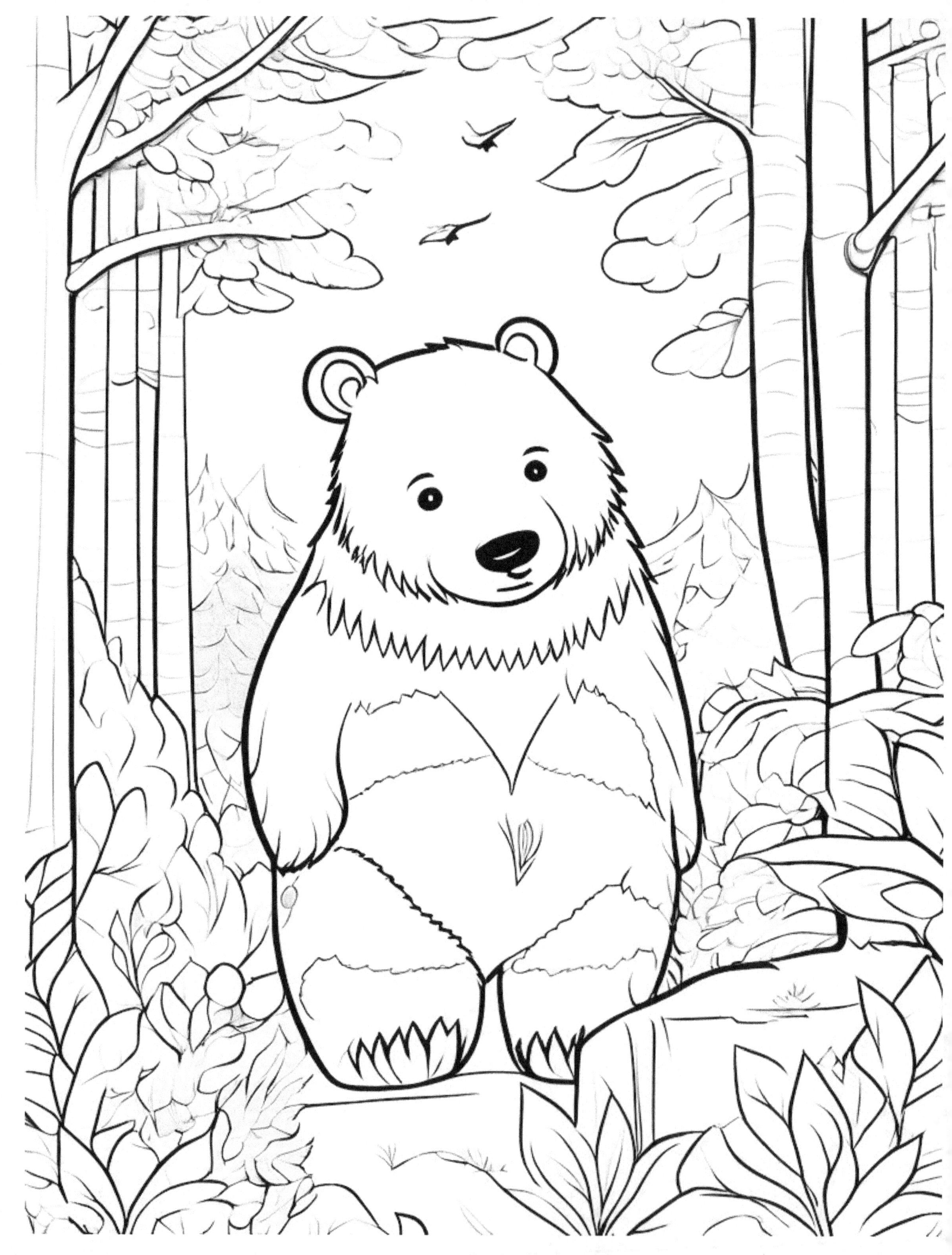

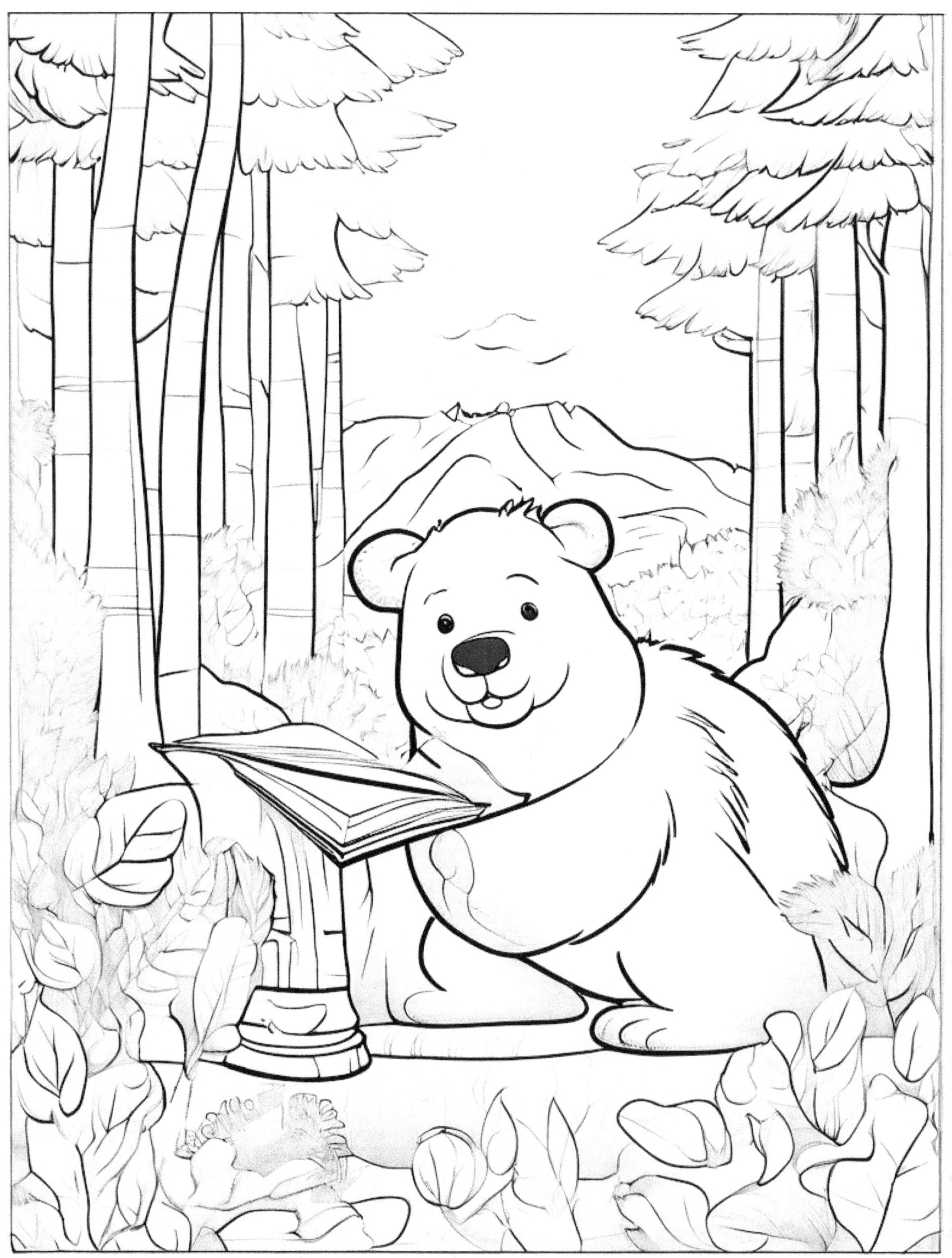

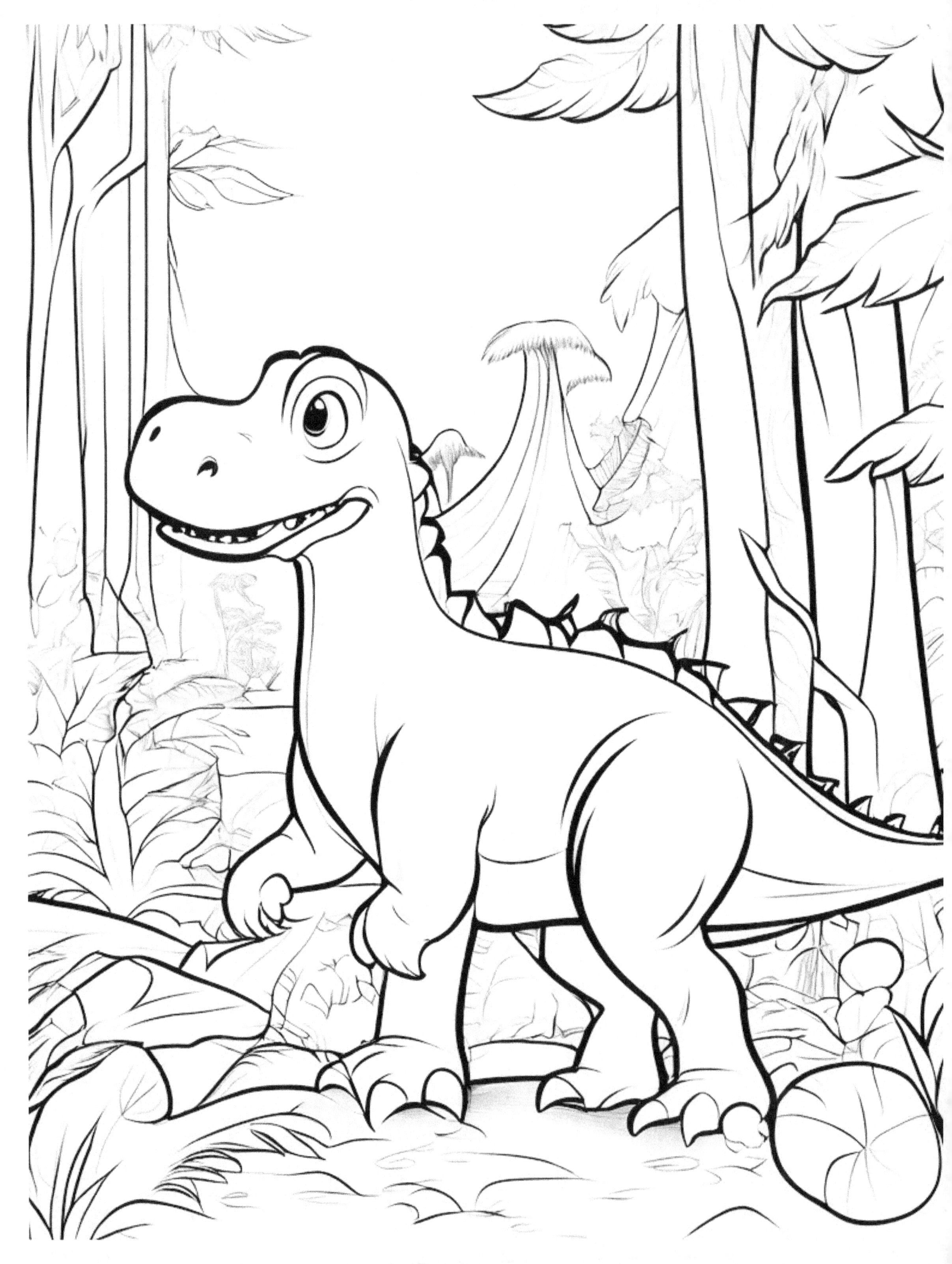

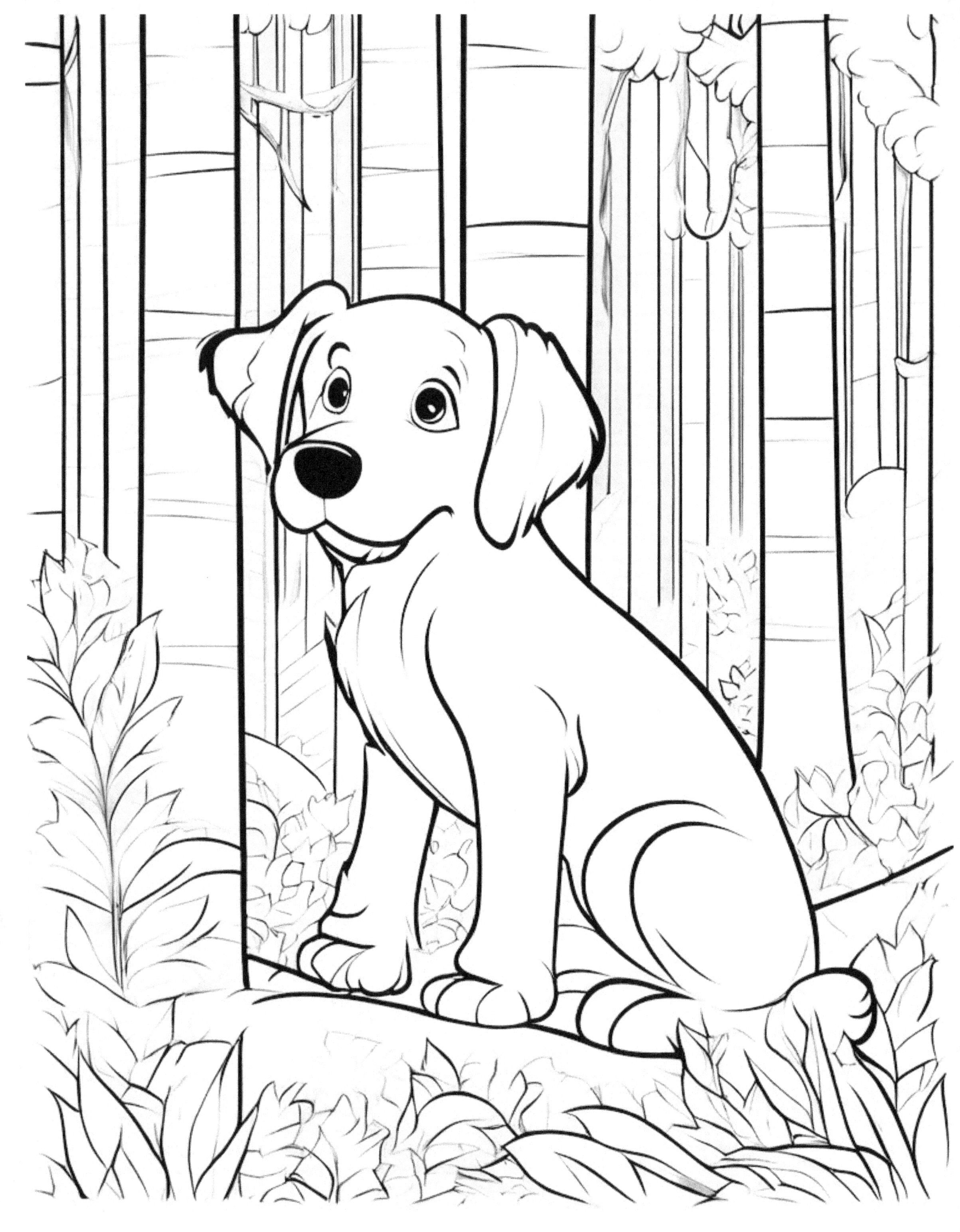